Praise for *The Discerning*

"Retirement is frightening, especially for those of us near—or at—retirement age, on at least three levels—it presages a potentially dramatic change in the remainder of our lives, it requires us to confront the last, or terminal, phase of our existence and, for attorneys, it forces us to recognize that we have been procrastinating about this critical subject for most of our professional lives. Now, there is a solution. Instead of continuing to procrastinate, read Julie Jason's excellent guide, *The Discerning Investor*. Written with true insight, understanding and an overarching goal of helping lawyers and their clients confront a difficult topic, this book provides a wealth of information in a readable, understandable and useful format that will warm the hearts of all lawyer-procrastinators. *If you read one book on retirement, this is the one, and you should read it now!*"

~ *Harvey L. Pitt, former SEC Chairman;*
CEO of Global Business Consultancy, Kalorama Partners, LLC

"As a consultant to law firms, I can give it to you straight: You've had a successful law career and you've built your nest egg. Don't screw it up in retirement. Read *The Discerning Investor* for its valuable tools to help organize priorities and focus those priorities on actionable steps. Julie has her own distinct conversational voice and way of making complex concepts come alive. The tone is very direct and devoid of 'investment-speak,' i.e., no jargon. Every partner of every large law firm should not only read *The Discerning Investor* for his or her own benefit, but also provide a copy to every new partner and associate."

~ *Peter Giuliani, Career law firm business consultant,*
Partner, Smock Law Firm Consultants (smocklawfirmconsultants.com).
Author of Passing the Torch Without Getting Burned, *ABA, 2013*

"As an investment management lawyer representing investment advisers and broker-dealers servicing primarily retail investors, I have seen it all. From overreaching sales practices and unfair marketing to outright fraud. *The Discerning Investor* lays out the law governing the investment advice industry and will help you make one of the most difficult decisions in your life—selecting a financial institution and financial adviser to help with your investments."

~Max Schatzow, Esq.,
Co-founder & Partner of RIA Lawyers, LLC

"As former Wall Street litigation counsel to a major broker-dealer, arbitrator, and mediator, and a life-long investor, I recommend Julie Jason's book to lawyers who are approaching retirement. If you are—or wish to be—a 'discerning' investor in your retirement, this book will serve you well."

~ Richard P. Ryder, Esq., Founder,
Securities Arbitration Commentator, Inc.

"Julie Jason's *The Discerning Investor* offers solid advice for retirees and pre-retirees. Julie takes much of the mystery out of personal portfolio management and helps the reader understand many of the mechanics without complexity."

~ Russell L. Abrahms, CPA, CPA to highly successful individuals,
families and businesses for more than 25 years

"Who would benefit from reading *The Discerning Investor*? A lawyer who wants to enjoy retirement having accumulated wealth the hard way, by working at it. There is more involved than meets the eye. It's more than picking stocks. It's more than working with a broker. Creating cash flow to support a lifestyle takes some time to organize. Strategy needs to be set (Chapter 7 is an eye-opener). Monitoring needs to follow. Choosing investment advisers takes some knowledge and due diligence. Freedom from conflicts of interest becomes more important. All of these factors come together in Julie Jason's *The Discerning Investor*, culminating in my two favorite chapters. Chapter 14 introduces an innovative "Know

Your Representative Rule." Chapter 15 takes readers through a creative self-assessment leading to getting to know yourself better as a retirement investor. Who should read this book? I can't think of any lawyer, young or old, who wouldn't benefit."

~ Manny Bernardo (retired attorney), Former Director of Employee Benefits Tax Services for Deloitte & Touche Tristate, Benefits Specialist Attorney, and Human Resources Benefits Executive

"As lawyers, we are always so busy keeping our clients on the straight and narrow that we sometimes neglect to tend our own gardens. Every good lawyer knows only too well what he or she does not know. We would never think to help our clients choose investments for their portfolios, as there are other professionals who specialize in that. But sometimes our clients want us to make recommendations. How do you pick the right investment professionals for your clients, or yourself? Too many of us rely on country club cronies, college classmates, people we meet at the gym, or (increasingly) online profiles we stumble across on social media, without even knowing if anyone's financial future should be trusted to them. Hats off to Julie Jason for finally demystifying the process of selecting an investment adviser, using new SEC Form CRS as a guide. *The Discerning Investor* will help you look beyond a professional's veneer and ferret out what is important that will help you or your client determine if he or she is the right fit. Any lawyer familiar with business due diligence will savor this book."

~ Cliff Ennico, lawyer, nationally syndicated columnist and author of 16 books, including The Crowdfunding Handbook *(HarperCollins 2016)*

"In *The Discerning Investor*, Julie Jason helps readers cut through the noise and hazards of investing and retirement planning. The issue for many is that we are overloaded with news of each day's market fluctuations and experts' opinions on how the day's economic and political events contributed. Julie Jason explains why smart investors take a steady, measured, long term approach. She walks us through important decisions and identifies pitfalls that can cause us to veer off course. For those interested in ways to measure portfolio composition and performance, she explains analytical tools professionals use. She lucidly describes the proper role and responsibility of financial advisers and provides a guide for finding the right financial firm and individual. It is never too early to think about retirement planning. *The Discerning Investor* is a road map to long term retirement planning success that everyone should read."

~ Clifford Alexander, Partner, K&L Gates

"Julie Jason's *The Discerning Investor* meticulously explains the various issues that must be considered when formulating a successful financial retirement plan. From identifying one's goal to the various options for achieving those goals, Julie has clearly articulated what one must consider with or without a financial advisor. For the uninformed, her words are informative when deciding whether or not they need a financial adviser and, if one is needed, what one should expect from an adviser upon which great reliance and trust will lie."

~ Jay Sandak,
Partner, Carmody, Torrance, Sandak & Hennessey LLP

"Selecting the right financial professional can be challenging, but new SEC disclosures are now available. Julie Jason uses her extensive knowledge and experience to highlight the key topics and questions to bring up when meeting with a current or prospective financial professional. This book provides you with the framework for determining whether that professional is right for you, or is someone you should avoid."

~Charles Rotblut, CFA, V.P., American Association of Individual Investors, Editor of the AAII Journal, *Author of* Better Good than Lucky: How Savvy Investors Create Fortune with the Risk-Reward Ratio *(Traders Press 2010)*

"Preparation helps avoid pitfalls. Julie Jason offers the reader a dose of "virtual valium" through stock market history and practical recommendations to help stop the nervous investor from allowing their emotions to become their retirement portfolio's worst enemy."

~Sam Stovall, Chief Investment Strategist, CFRA Research, Author of The Seven Rules of Wall Street: Crash-Tested Investment Strategies That Beat the Market *(McGraw-Hill Education 2009)*

AMERICAN**BAR**ASSOCIATION
Senior Lawyers Division

The Discerning Investor

Personal Portfolio Management in Retirement for Lawyers (and Their Clients)

JULIE JASON, JD, LLM

Dedication

To Joanna, Penelope, and Peter, and their parents, Ilona and Onur

Olivia and Margot, and their parents, Leila and Mark

GJP and RSP

and my loving (and very patient) Bill

Foreword

Stephen E. Seckler, Esq.

Retirement today is very different than it was 50 years ago. People are living longer, and lawyers, like many other knowledge workers, have the ability to work well into their sixties and seventies and beyond. Supreme Court Justice Ruth Bader Ginsburg was productive well into her late eighties.

But for many lawyers, continuing to work is a default option rather than something that has been carefully planned out. Part of the reason is that lawyers have very strong professional identities. Part of the reason is finances.

As high-income earners, many lawyers fear that they won't have enough money to last them throughout retirement. That fear needs to be addressed before decisions can be made.

From my perspective as a career coach, I see lawyers creating meaningful and productive "next chapters" of their lives. A crucial part of this is to look at finances, a challenging topic well laid out by Julie Jason, JD, LLM, in *The Discerning Investor: Personal Portfolio Management in Retirement for Lawyers (and Their Clients)*.

Given how long many Americans are now living, taking the time to prepare to finance your possibly lengthy retirement is essential in making a successful career transition. Finances should really be the first step in *any* transition planning.

To help you in your journey, Julie has created a great starting point. In this book, she walks you through the key concepts and considerations needed to create a viable financial program for your retirement, whatever that retirement looks like.

The Discerning Investor prepares you to avoid miscues and take advantage of opportunities to ensure that the wealth you created during your career will now work for you in your third chapter based on your personal preferences.

Planning your future has many dimensions. Maybe you will become a mentor to younger lawyers at your firm or spend more time doing pro bono work. Perhaps you will get active on nonprofit boards. Maybe you will decide to pick up the guitar that you really enjoyed playing as a teenager and a young adult (the instrument that has been sitting in your attic for 30 years). Perhaps you will spend more time traveling, studying religion, or writing the screenplay that has been in your head for several decades.

If you are healthy, it can be an exciting time of life. Figuring out how you will make it all work financially is an important first step.

Stephen E. Seckler, Esq. (stephen.seckler@counseltocounsel.com) *is president of Seckler Attorney Coaching. As "Counsel to Counsel" over the last three decades, he has coached hundreds of attorneys through career transitions and helped hundreds of lawyers to grow their income.* Counsel to Counsel *is his website and podcast. His program,* The Next Stage, *is for senior attorneys thinking about "what comes next."*

Contents

Part II: Personal Portfolio Management Principles 49

Introduction

The *Discerning Investor* is a book for investors
who happen to be lawyers, written by a lawyer who
also happens to be "investment counsel."[1]

Take a moment to consider your financial situation.

What is your sense of security about having enough saved for the future? How should you invest a lifetime's worth of savings to preserve wealth while supporting your lifestyle for the length of retirement? What are your thoughts about how to plan and act in a way that protects you and your family, perhaps leaving a legacy for heirs or charitable bequests? What if you are single and become incapacitated? What if you are married and predecease your spouse or partner?

Is investing in retirement any different from how you invest today? Are the demands the same? Are the risks the same? Are the goals the same? Is *anything* the same?

The Investor Advisory Committee to the U.S. Securities and Exchange Commission (SEC) sees retirement as a "critical juncture in an investor's life" . . . often accompanied with "irrevocable decisions."[2]

Agreed.

---

1. Investment counsel is a type of investment adviser that, in layman's terms, focuses on creating and managing portfolios tailored to the needs of individual clients. My firm, Jackson, Grant Investment Advisers, Inc. (www.jacksongrantus.com), acts in that fiduciary capacity, specializing in personal portfolio management in retirement.

2. Referencing the SEC Investor Advisory Committee's phraseology in "Regarding Proposed Regulation Best Interest, Form CRS, and Investment Advisers Act Fiduciary Guidance," U.S. Securities and Exchange Commission's Investor Advisory Committee, November 7, 2018, 4. https://www.sec.gov/spotlight/investor-advisory-committee-2012/recommendation-on-proposed-reg-bi.pdf.

Nobel Prize winner and professor William F. Sharpe (Stanford University) calls creating retirement income "the nastiest, hardest problem in finance" to solve.[3]

So true.

If one is unprepared . . .

* * *

To save you time as you tackle the intricacies of preparing for the future, in this book,[4] I'll share what I have seen contribute to (and detract from) "retirement security," over my 30+ years in the financial services industry.

Had I not started my Wall Street career as a lawyer preparing proxy statements, working on prospectus disclosures, and participating in industry committees, I doubt I would have developed the lawyerly traits—skepticism being most important—needed to manage retirement portfolios within a framework packed with *uncertainties*, both in the client's life and in the markets.

My goal is to give you the tools to organize and plan for the future in a way that is uniquely yours.

Starting Point. Part I of *The Discerning Investor* lays out a conceptual framework for managing a retirement portfolio with an emphasis on anticipating and thus avoiding mistakes such as misjudging risk. I think you will agree that retirement is not the ideal time to learn through trial

---

3. Barry Ritholtz, "Tackling the 'Nastiest, Hardest Problem in Finance,'" *Bloomberg Quint* (June 5, 2017), https://www.bloombergquint.com/onweb/tackling-the-nastiest -hardest-problem-in-finance. Also, read Sharpe's "Retirement Income Analysis" (2019), http://web.stanford.edu/~wfsharpe/RISMAT/.

4. There are many books on the subject of how to make investment decisions as a self-directed investor who uses a broker-dealer for recommendations and execution, including purchasing retirement income products such as annuities. I'll share three examples: William O'Neil's *How to Make Money in Stocks* (first published in 1995); John Bogle's *The Little Book of Common Sense Investing: The Only Way to Guarantee Your Fair Share of Stock Market Returns* (2007; 2017), and, of course, the classic *The Intelligent Investor* (first published in 1949) by Benjamin Graham, which included a chapter (4) titled, "The Investor and His Advisers." In addition, my book, *The Retirement Survival Guide* (2009; 2017), an update of my earlier book, *The AARP Retirement Survival Guide*, is for a broader audience than *The Discerning Investor* and includes a systematic review of products that create retirement income. In contrast, *The Discerning Investor* focuses on the more strategic approach required when creating and tending to a retirement portfolio, led by a registered investment adviser (whether stand-alone or dual registrant) specializing in personal portfolio management as that term is defined in Chapter 1.

and *error*. You'll be introduced to "personal portfolio management," a phrase that captures what's involved when investing in retirement.

Chapters 1 and 2 will help set the stage. Chapters 3 and 4 are heavy with market data that you will either enjoy or skim.

Strategy. In Part II of the book, we'll talk about how to bring "you" into the portfolio equation. This discussion will help you merge market knowledge with your personal situation and make use of tools that can help you judge how you are doing. The ultimate goal is developing a strategy that addresses your situation.

Self-assessment. Before deciding on a course of action, it is important to recognize that there is no one-size-fits-all retirement solution. For example, the 4 percent safe withdrawal rule[5] that you may be familiar with does not apply to everyone (and was never intended to do so). Every retiree I've ever met is different from every other. Finances, time horizons, health and family situations differ, as do needs and wants—and hopes and fears. A customized *plan* is the answer, not only to avoid miscues but also to accommodate your family's unique needs, more so if you have significant assets or complex holdings.

Execution. The actual execution of your strategic plan is subject to another type of risk: the risk of assuming that maintaining the status quo will serve you well in retirement. That may not be the case.

Part III of the book will help you make an informed decision, after introducing what a lawyer will want to know about financial services choices—before embarking on retirement. But let me put things into perspective now. It comes down to this: You will have two choices. One: retain a firm to structure and manage your portfolio.[6] Two: take on the management role yourself while using a brokerage firm to execute trades.[7]

In either case, your search is now (after June 2020) made much easier with Form CRS (Client Relationship Summary), the subject of Chapter 12. The CRS is a two-page (or four-page) disclosure document mandated by the U.S. Securities and Exchange Commission (SEC) for firms regulated under two sets of laws: the Securities Exchange Act of 1934

---

5. Chapter 5.

6. This service is provided by a *registered investment adviser* (whether a stand-alone investment adviser or dual registrant), as discussed in Part III of the book.

7. This service is provided by a *broker-dealer* (whether a stand-alone broker-dealer or a dual registrant), as discussed in Part III of the book.

(regulating brokers) and the Investment Advisers Act of 1940 (regulating investment advisers).[8]

As someone who has experience as a lawyer and an executive, both on Wall Street with a broker-dealer and on Main Street with an investment adviser, I see the CRS as a critical tool. The CRS allows one to quickly grasp *what a client experience might be like* based on the firm's service offerings and the conflicts imbedded in the way the firm does business. That's not something that most people are able to do on their own (until now). Moreover, some may not be motivated to pursue this type of inquiry. That is, one can easily assume that (1) every "financial adviser"[9] is trusted to be acting in a fiduciary capacity with no self-interest in the equation (not so) and (2) that all financial advisers *manage* retirement portfolios (also not so).

Part IV returns to self-discovery through two new self-assessment tools[10] created to move beyond the status quo to the transition into retirement investing. Your law background will help you, as this phase of life calls for analysis, advanced planning, and an understanding of not only the law that governs the different types of financial firms *that you might retain* but also the business practices that define the relationship between you and the financial firm *that you do retain.*

The desired outcome is for you to be able to feel *prepared* for retirement *on your own terms.*

* * *

A Note to Lawyers Serving as Fiduciaries or Referrers

Lawyers are in a unique position of trust, serving others as counselors and advocates. As such, you may be asked to act as trustee or to advise clients, family, friends, or colleagues on their investments. Parts I and II of the book will be particularly helpful to you when acting in those capacities.

---

8. Note that some firms are registered as investment advisers (stand-alone advisers); some are registered as broker-dealers (stand-alone broker-dealers); some are registered as both investment advisers and broker-dealers (dual registrants).

9. Regulations effective in 2020 no longer permit financial representatives to call themselves financial "advisers" unless they are regulated under the Investment Advisers Act of 1940 (the "Advisers Act"). See Part III of the book for a more detailed discussion.

10. See Chapters 14 and 15.

If you are asked by someone for a referral to a financial firm or financial professional, Part III of this book will help you with your due diligence in the current regulatory environment, with its new set of standards and disclosures. Part IV will help the person to whom you are making a referral personalize his or her own selection criteria.

* * *

Additional Material

Digital Downloads and Suggested Reading

You may benefit from the downloadable bonus content accessible here: www.juliejason.com/discerninginvestor/. This download pack includes files for your clients on integrating financial and estate plans, which includes a discussion of the importance of correctly titling investment accounts; a review of red flags that can identify potential financial exploitation of seniors; and a discussion of Post-SECURE Act considerations for those who inherit Individual Retirement Arrangements (IRAs).

At the end of the book, I've also included a suggested reading list should you wish to pursue certain topics further.

PART I
Personal Portfolio Management and The Markets

In Part I of this book, I will introduce a way to prepare for retirement with the ultimate goal of getting organized, enough so to envision the potential structure for an appropriate retirement portfolio. We'll discuss some of the more important introductory concepts that underpin the formation of a portfolio, the foundation from which investment strategies flow. I'll share market information and insights from experts to enable you to get a sense of how to understand and manage the risk that is inevitably a part of every investor's life.

Note: The market data in this book has to be understood in context. The information presented is not intended to constitute an investment recommendation for, or advice to, any specific person. Returns may not be repeated in the future; past performance is no guarantee of future results. Different market periods than those discussed produce different results. Index data, such as for the S&P 500 Index, is not reflective of actual investor experience, since an investor would need to account for fees, expenses, and sales charges with the purchase of an index fund that sought to replicate the index. With these caveats in mind, it is important to look at historical trends. They may or may not repeat, but it is essential to know what they have been as we position for the future.

Chapter 1
Introducing Personal Portfolio Management

No matter your age, you will need to create a strategy that will help guide your investment decisions through each stage of life and prepare you for the decades that define retirement. At stake is your own and your family's security. How you formulate and execute that strategy depends in large part on you. Retirement investing is a very *personal* exercise.

Thinking strategically will lead to an action plan that tackles the more complex investment outcomes desired by retirees—creating *lifelong* financial security for yourself and your family, and potentially creating a legacy for either your heirs or charities, or both. Let's put a name on this exercise and define it.

Defining Personal Portfolio Management

I like the term "personal portfolio management"[1] to capture the idea that a retirement portfolio is unique to the individual, and requires a long-term commitment, much like running a family business.

The term "portfolio" has special meaning. In the words of Nobel Prize–winning economist and father of portfolio management Harry M. Markowitz, a portfolio is "more than a long list of good stocks and bonds . . . [it is a] balanced whole [that provides] protections and opportunities with respect to a wide range of contingencies."[2]

---

1. Professor George W. Trivoli wrote a book titled *Personal Portfolio Management: Fundamentals and Strategies*; however, that book is about the basics of investing.
2. Harry M. Markowitz, Portfolio Selection: Efficient Diversification of Investments 3 (Yale Univ. Press 1959/1970). Markowitz did not apply his theories to individuals.

A "personal portfolio" is goal-oriented, meaning it focuses on your personal and unique situation and addresses the goals you want to achieve now and in the future.

"Management" is the process of planning, executing, and, equally important, *monitoring* progress against goals, to adjust for changing markets, needs, and circumstances over the decades that comprise the investor's lifetime. This approach may be new to you (if you have never retired before) or old hat (if you have experience running a long-term enterprise).

At this point, I'd like to have you think about your personal situation as you plan your next move. We need to discuss time horizon considerations, your personal role in managing your retirement wealth, and how to assess financial expertise in order to match your particular needs.

Time Horizon

Not too long ago, a retirement timeline assumed you lived into your seventies, supported by a pension and Social Security retirement benefits. Today, pensions are almost nonexistent, life expectancies are greater, and financial success is a function of sound wealth creation and management. Moreover, in the best situations, our timelines (see Figure 1.1) extend beyond our lifetimes, to benefit heirs and charities.

It's important to undertand that your retirement planning will encompass a much longer period of time than you might first envision.

Figure 1.1 Time Horizon

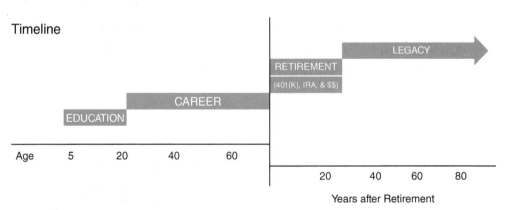

Source: Jackson, Grant.

Your Personal Role

In my experience, lawyers, accountants, business owners, corporate officers, and other successful individuals have a number of brokerage accounts, retirement accounts, and even financial relationships that have served them well. At some point (perhaps now), the strategic objectives of retirement push for the need to think things through with a fresh outlook, with the goal of developing a comprehensive retirement plan, one that runs smoothly and is easy for you to manage. As you look to retire, consider these questions:

- Will my current methods of investing serve me well in my retirement, which will hopefully last decades, and serve my legacy goals thereafter?
- What more do I need to know to be successful when dealing with retirement finances?
- Do I want to be in charge of multiple accounts?
- How do I get reorganized as I move into retirement?
- If I have gaps in my knowledge, how can I fill those gaps?
- How do I measure success with a retirement portfolio?
- How do I avoid mistakes?
- How do I define my job as an investor in retirement?
- Can I, should I, delegate the role to someone else?

Once you have clarity on your goals and capabilities, you can make a well-grounded choice about how to manage your retirement portfolio. You may decide to retain expertise or, if you have the training, interest, and time, you may decide to tackle the job yourself.

Four More Points to Ponder

These four points may help provide additional context:

1. **You have a retirement income gap.** If pensions and Social Security do not cover your living expenses, you have a "retirement income gap."[3] This means you will need to turn your savings into a cash

---

3. To calculate your retirement income gap, answer the following questions: How much are you spending on an annual basis? How much Social Security and pension

flow stream that will not only last a lifetime but also outpace inflation and taxes and prepare you for the unexpected. You might also
want to leave a legacy for children or charity, or both. This is a
big-picture activity that needs to be conceptualized, coordinated,
and managed over time. Having a retirement income gap increases
the need for vigilance and planning and calls for organizing multiple accounts into a consolidated portfolio. (Someone who does
not have a retirement income gap has a significantly simpler investment challenge.)

2. **Your spouse/partner is not interested in investing.** If your spouse or
partner is not interested in making investment decisions with you,
then managing your own portfolio would create risk for him or her
in the event you become incapacitated. To mitigate that risk, your
spouse/partner would need to understand, among other things:

   • How a retirement portfolio should be structured; whether the
   economy and other news events should trigger buy, sell, and hold
   decisions; and the effect of taxes and inflation. The ability to
   make these assessments takes knowledge, typically gained over
   time.

   • How living expenses are covered. What are the sources, such as
   Social Security and pension income, cash produced by investments, or other holdings? And when is it time to redirect or
   reconsider how you are producing and spending cash flow, after
   inflation and taxes? The ability to either prepare or review this
   information is essential in structuring a proper portfolio.

   • How to assess conflicts of interest imbedded in financial relationships. To understand conflicts takes experience and the ability to
   scrutinize disclosure documents.

   • How to interact with financial professionals who may have close
   long-standing relationships (should all recommendations be
   accepted; when and how to say "no"). This takes judgment, wisdom, and a dose of healthy skepticism.

---

income are you taking in on an annual basis? What's the difference between the two?
That's the retirement income gap.

3. **You are single.** If you are single, you will need to settle on who you can mobilize (children, siblings, friends, trustees) to make investment decisions for you in the event of incapacity. (The points just made in number 2 apply here as well.)

4. **You have limited time or interest.** If you would rather be pursuing other interests in your retirement, the effort and skills to manage a retirement portfolio can be a burden. Health issues, now or in the future, might limit your ability to make sound investment decisions. This is particularly important to address sooner rather than later, especially if you are finding your ability to handle the management role more taxing than you would like. This is not uncommon as one advances through one's retirement years.

If you are in any of these situations, think long and hard about the benefits of retaining expertise to manage your retirement portfolio. Who might those experts be?

Financial Expertise

Briefly, the U.S. Securities and Exchange Commission (SEC)[4] regulates financial service providers based on their business models under two separate statutes, one governing the giving of investment advice,[5] the other governing investment transactions.[6] You'll have a better feel for the type of expertise to retain as you read through this book; your choice depends entirely on your personal preferences and how much you want to be involved in the personal portfolio management process.

---

4. Note that state securities authorities also regulate financial firms. For example, investment advisory firms that manage less than $100 million are excluded from SEC registration. Instead, these smaller firms generally register with state securities regulators under the laws of the states in which they do business. At the end of 2019, there were 17,000 state-registered investment advisers. See NASAA's annual report at https://www.nasaa.org/wp-content/uploads/2020/04/2020-IA-Section-Report-FINAL.pdf. NASAA is the North American Securities Administrators Association. See https://www.nasaa.org/industry-resources/investment-advisers/state-investment-adviser-registration-information/.

5. The Investment Advisers Act of 1940 (the "Advisers Act").

6. The Securities Exchange Act of 1934 (the "1934 Act").

Key Takeaways

For most people of means, retirement investing is very different from investing before retirement. The horizon is decades long, multiple goals need to be met, and spouses may not be as interested as you are in making financial decisions. Perhaps there are charitable interests that need to be addressed; potential mistakes need to be understood, and avoided; a plan needs to be considered, structured, and implemented—all executed, hopefully, within a framework of calm seas, sunny skies, and smooth sailing. The big message is: This is not the time to learn through trial and error.

Now, let's turn to what you can expect to experience in the financial markets, with a skeptic's view on what can go wrong, so that miscues can be avoided.

Chapter 2
Avoiding Mistakes: A Historical Perspective on the Stock Market

This chapter's review of historical stock market returns exposes potential mistakes that an investor can make. For example, in retirement, sensitivity to market downturns can lead to the mistake of capitulating at the wrong time. We saw such a period in 2020, when the coronavirus market[1] understandably created uncertainty in the minds of retirees who depended on their retirement assets to cover living expenses. The natural tendency would be to sell stocks to go to cash to protect against a further decline. However, students of the market would tell you that it's far better to hold steady unless, of course, assets are not structured properly for retirement. (In Part II (Chapters 5 through 8), we'll cover how to make sure your assets *are* structured properly.)

With that in mind, in this chapter and Chapters 3 and 4, we will review market data to prepare you for markets that you will inevitably experience.

My point in providing market information is simply this: "By studying the past, one can make inferences about the future. While the actual events that occurred . . . will not be repeated, the event-types of that period can be expected to recur," quoting Roger Ibbotson's SBBI Yearbook.[2] The Yearbook is a standard reference for the capital market returns that I

---

1. The coronavirus bear, a decline of 34 percent, lasted from February 19, 2020, through March 23, 2020.

2. Roger G. Ibbotson, 2020 SBBI® Yearbook Stocks, Bonds, Bills, and Inflation: U.S. Capital Markets Performance by Asset Class 1926–2019, at 2-1 (Duff & Phelps 2020).

will be using throughout Part I of this book. Ibbotson[3] is Professor in the Practice Emeritus of Finance at Yale School of Management.

This point of view is consistent with investment experts, as noted by the CFA Institute.[4] When the Institute asked investment professionals, "How important is knowledge of financial/economic history to your success?" a vast majority (77 percent) rated it "very important."[5] The CFA Institute issues the CFA® credential, which is recognized globally as the gold standard investment credential.[6]

Learning from the Past

As an investor, you must be prepared to weather market volatility. Consequently, before you construct a retirement portfolio, it helps to have an appreciation of long-term and short-term stock market history.

Why long term? Retirement portfolios need to last a lifetime (and beyond, if leaving a legacy is a goal). Why short term? Investors are susceptible to veering off course when volatility strikes. This is not helpful in retirement, whether the temptation is chasing a high-flying bull market or selling during a large downside move.

Before introducing market data, let me share the two situations that are most risky for a retiree who has created retirement wealth, but never had the experience of retiring before. Let's consider two types of markets, a bull market and a bear market.

A Conservative Retiree Reacting to a Bull Market

I'd like to tell you a story that happened at the top of the Internet Bubble, in January 2000. "John," a conservative retiree with a balanced portfolio, asked me if he should sell his holdings to buy internet stocks. At the time, returns for the highest-flying stocks were dazzling everyone. The question I posed was, "What about risk?"

---

3. https://som.yale.edu/faculty/roger-g-ibbotson.

4. The CFA Institute is recognized as a leading global association for investment management professionals focused on education, research, and best practices. www.cfainstitute.org.

5. Desi Allevato, *Should Financial History Matter to Investors?*, CFA INST. MAG., Sept./Oct. 2015, at 17.

6. CFA stands for Chartered Financial Analyst® designation (also called CFA® Charterholder).

"This market is different," John replied. "Technology and internet stocks will continue to go up. My friends are making money, and I don't want to be left behind."

This gentleman's outlook reflected the then-current wisdom: This was a "new economy" where people began to think that new rules applied. When a normally conservative person buys into a current fad, it is a sign of a speculative market.

A few months later, the NASDAQ peaked (at the close of March 10, 2000), falling 78 percent by the October 9, 2002 close.[7]

The incident made me think of a story about Joseph Kennedy, Wall Street financier and father of U.S. President John F. Kennedy. He is said to have sold his stocks just before the Great Crash of 1929, after his shoeshine boy offered him a stock tip. Bernard Baruch, a successful stockbroker, investor, and presidential adviser, had a similar insight:

> When beggars and shoeshine boys, barbers and beauticians can tell you how to get rich it is time to remind yourself that there is no more dangerous illusion than the belief that one can get something for nothing.[8]

History teaches us that major technological advances fueled speculative fever in the past. In the 1920s, the automobile and the radio were the technological wonders of the time and still play a major role in our lives. It took 33 years, however, for Radio Corporation of America (RCA) to recover after it reached its peak in 1929.[9]

The same was true of the late-1960s bull market. Dominated by the "Nifty Fifty,"[10] the S&P 500 Index was driven by consumer goods and technology stocks. However, higher inflation, expansionary monetary policy, and increased oil costs led to two bear markets, first in 1969–1970

---

7. NASDAQ Composite Index (COMP), WSJ Markets, https://www.wsj.com/market-data/quotes/index/COMP/historical-prices.

8. Kenneth Fisher, 100 Minds That Made the Market 376 (John Wiley & Sons 1993/2007).

9. ISL Daily Stock Price Index: New York Stock Exchange. 1964: January February March. Standard and Poors Corporation, 1964, at 239.

10. Twenty-nine of the Nifty Fifty are still public companies. Eleven Nifty Fifty companies are in the top 50 of the S&P 500 Index. Charles Rotblut, *Are Any of the Nifty 50 Stocks Still Nifty?*, AAII (May 23, 2019), https://www.aaii.com/investor-update/article/Are-Any-of-the-Nifty-50-Stocks-Still-Nifty.

and again in 1973–1974.[11] During the latter period, stock market aver-
ages dropped about 50 percent.[12]

Boom markets create a careless attitude on the part of investors who,
inspired by wishful thinking and the stories of fortunes being made by
others, close their eyes to risk. Sadly, many who enter the fray late in the
game suffer large declines in the value of their holdings. To the uniniti-
ated, bull markets come with hidden dangers. Like the sirens of legend,
they can lure people into treacherous waters. When we see such markets
again—which we will—be alert. Beware of being tempted by the fad of
the day.

A Conservative Retiree Reacting to a Bear Market

Retirees (indeed, all investors) need to avoid the natural urge to second-
guess the direction of the market. Moving to cash (selling stock holdings)
at the wrong time dramatically affects results.

The coronavirus bear market is a good example of a frightening experience that caused those who capitulated to lock in losses.

While no one knew it at the time, this bear market turned out to be the
shortest on record, lasting only 1.1 months, from February 19, 2020, to
March 23, 2020, after declining 34 percent. The bull market that preceded
it started in 2009, lasting 131.5 months, the longest bull market run in history since the 1920s.[13]

Market Timing

Selling in order to protect against further declines is a natural reaction
for a retiree who has amassed retirement wealth. Unexpected events like
COVID-19 can result in panic selling during a sudden drop in the stock
market. The move, however, can create a worse outcome by locking in
losses.

---

11. IBBOTSON, *supra* note 2, at 11-12, Exhibit 11.8 Longest Declines in US Stock
Market History. *See also* Federal Reserve History: *The Great Inflation 1965–1982*,
November 22, 2013, https://www.federalreservehistory.org/essays/great-inflation.

12. IBBOTSON, *supra* note 2, at 11-12, Exhibit 11.8 Longest Declines in US Stock
Market History.

13. Data Sam Stovall, Chief Investment Strategist, CFRA Research, *S&P 500 Bull
Markets Since 1921* (Jan. 4, 2021). Sam Stovall is the author of *The Seven Rules of Wall
Street* (McGraw Hill, 2009).

If the intent is to get back in at the right time, when is the right time? Not knowing the answer leads to cash sitting on the sidelines during upward movements of the market.

Even being out of the market for a few days sets one up to reduce returns, sometimes significantly. To illustrate, let me share J.P. Morgan's[14] market timing study that considered the 20-year period ending 2020.

Missing even a small percentage of trading days significantly affected results. As Table 2-1 illustrates, if you were fully invested in the market (through an S&P 500 Index fund) during the 20-year period (2002–2021), you would have made 7.5 percent annualized. If you were not invested during the best 60 days, you would have lost 6.8 percent annualized, a swing of 14.3 percentage points. That point bears repeating. By missing only 1 percent of the trading days during the period, an investor's return in an S&P 500 Index Fund *resulted in a loss of 6.8 percent instead of a gain of 7.5 percent.*[15]

Table 2-1 Missing Out on Market Moves

2000 through 2020	Days	Total Return
Missing best	60 days	–6.8%
Missing best	50 days	–5.2%
Missing best	40 days	–3.4%
Missing best	30 days	–1.5%
Missing best	20 days	0.7%
Missing best	10 days	3.4%
Missing no days	0 days	7.5%

This is an extremely important point for any investor to understand, more so a retiree. A retiree with a well-defined investment strategy is better served than one who is in favor of timing the market, regardless of whether the attempt is to make more or to lose less.

---

14. Data from *Guide to Retirement*, J.P. Morgan Asset Management, 44 (2022), https://am.jpmorgan.com/content/dam/jpm-am-aem/global/en/insights/retirement-insights/guide-to-retirement-us.pdf. This study shows S&P 500 Index returns, which illustrates an investor's experience with an S&P 500 Index Fund before expenses and fees.

15. There are just over 5,000 trading days in a 20-year period.

Lessons from Difficult Market Periods

While the coronavirus bear market is useful to review, if we go just a little bit further back in history, we find even more illuminating examples. There is no better time period to study than the 2000–2009 decade. In that relatively short period, we saw a heady boom (the Internet Bubble) come abruptly to an end in 2000, then a subsequent rise in the market from 2002 to 2008, with a shift in market leadership from internet to financial stocks. This was followed by a spectacular financial meltdown as subprime mortgages defaulted, making related investments worthless. After 158 years in business, Lehman Brothers declared bankruptcy in September of 2008 and the federal government entered the marketplace with bailouts and government ownership. We also saw the real estate boom come to an end and the gold market take off.

During that decade, the market as measured by the Dow Jones Industrial Average Index ("the Dow" or index symbol "DJI") peaked at 14,165 on October 9, 2007, and bottomed at 6,547 on March 9, 2009, posting a dramatic drop of about 54 percent.[16] During the height of the financial panic, over a two-month period from September 15, 2008 (when Lehman Brothers filed for bankruptcy), to November 20, 2008, the Dow lost over 30 percent.[17] Down days followed down days. The market had absolutely no footing. Investors were not stepping up to buy—recognizing that would have been like trying to catch a falling sword.

Government support, more information, and the passage of time helped the markets recover. By the end of 2009, the Dow was up 59 percent to 10,428 from the March 9, 2009, bottom of 6,547.[18] Two years after the bottom, by March 31, 2011, the Dow had risen to 12,320, up 88 percent from the March 9, 2009, low, still shy of, but pretty close to, its October 9, 2007, peak. By the end of March 2013, the Dow was trading in pre-crisis territory.[19]

---

    16. NYSE. (2007). *Dow Jones Industrial Average (DJIA)*, retrieved from https://www.wsj.com/market-data/quotes/index/US/DJIA?mod=mdstrip.

    17. NYSE. (2008). *Dow Jones Industrial Average (DJIA)*, retrieved from https://www.wsj.com/market-data/quotes/index/US/DJIA?mod=mdstrip.

    18. NYSE. (2009). *Dow Jones Industrial Average (DJIA)*, retrieved from https://www.wsj.com/market-data/quotes/index/US/DJIA?mod=mdstrip.

    19. NYSE, *supra* note 16.

Flash Crashes

While the madness came to an end in March of 2009, we still saw after-shocks. From 2:41:00 p.m. through 2:45:27 p.m. on May 6, 2010, we experienced a "flash crash," when individual stocks and exchange traded funds (ETFs) fell by 5 percent to 15 percent in five minutes. A matter of minutes later, by 3:00 p.m., most stocks and ETFs had recovered.[20]

May 6, 2010 started with negative news on Greek debt levels. Later in the day, a large mutual fund "initiated a program to sell a total of 75,000 E-mini contracts (valued at approximately $4.1 billion) as a hedge to an existing equity position."[21] (The E-mini contract tracks the S&P 500 Index.) The mutual fund used an automated execution algorithm to sell the contracts at 9 percent of the trading volume without regard to time or price. As a result of the large demand, the pressure to sell at any cost fed on itself and pushed prices lower.

Regulators attributed the 2010 flash crash to the "new dynamics of the electronic markets that now characterize trading in equity and related exchange traded derivatives."[22] The SEC set up pauses for single stocks on top of the circuit breakers that had been in place after October 19, 1987 (also known as Black Monday), when the market lost more than 20 percent in one day.[23] In 2012, the SEC reduced the market decline percentage thresholds from 10 percent to 7 percent.[24]

There was another flash crash on August 24, 2015. Before the U.S. market opened, the Chinese Shanghai Composite Index dropped 8.5 percent, prompting U.S. traders to sell as soon as the market was open. By

---

20. Findings Regarding the Market Events of May 6, 2010: Report of the Staffs of the CFTC and SEC to the Joint Advisory Committee on Emerging Regulatory Issues, U.S. Commodity Futures Trading Comm'n and the U.S. Sec. & Exch. Comm'n, Sept. 30, 2021, at 4, https://www.sec.gov/news/studies/2010/marketevents-report.pdf.

21. *Id.* at 2.

22. *Summary Report of the Joint CFTC-SEC Advisory Committee: Recommendations Regarding Regulatory Responses to the Market Events of May 6, 2010*, U.S. Sec. & Exch. Comm'n 2, https://www.sec.gov/spotlight/sec-cftcjointcommittee/021811-report.pdf.

23. *Id.* at 3.

24. *Investor Bulletin: Measures to Address Market Volatility*, July 1, 2012, U.S. Sec. & Exch. Comm'n (last modified Jan. 4, 2016), https://www.sec.gov/oiea/investor-alerts-bulletins/investor-alerts-circuitbreakersbulletinhtm.html. In 2012, the SEC refined the triggers and halt times for the market circuit breakers.

9:35 a.m., only about half of the stocks on the New York Stock Exchange (NYSE) were open for trading. This meant that certain ETFs containing those stocks could not be priced accurately. As a result, an ETF designed to track the S&P 500's performance (SPY) fell around 7.8 percent from the previous day's closing price;[25] an S&P 500 dividend ETF (SDY) fell by 38 percent.[26] Both of these ETFs recovered back to a normal price range by the end of the day. The market circuit breakers did not work because the SPX (S&P 500 Index) was only down 5.2 percent, which did not meet the -7 percent threshold.[27]

Bear Markets

For an investor, the prospect of a bear market understandably causes anxiety. But bulls and bears are a natural function of a free market economy. As the economy expands or contracts, so do financial markets. The stock market will survive through the ups and downs that are sure to follow; the stock market will not go to zero.

History demonstrates that bear market periods have been shorter than bull markets, as can be seen from Table 2-2. From 1926 through December 2020, the average bear market lasted 16 months or 1.3 years,[28] with an average loss of 38 percent. The average bull market over the same time period lasted 51 months or 4.2 years, with an average gain of 162 percent.[29]

---

25. *SEC Research Note: Equity Market Volatility on August 24, 2015*, U.S. Sec. & Exch. Comm'n 1 (Dec. 2015), https://www.sec.gov/marketstructure/research/equity _market_volatility.pdf.

26. Chris Dieterich, *The Great ETF Debacle Explained*, Barron's (Sept. 5, 2015), https://www.barrons.com/articles/the-great-etf-debacle-explained-1441434195.

27. *SEC Research Note, supra* note 25, at 16.

28. The shortest bear market lasted only 1.1 months, the coronavirus bear of 2020.

29. Stovall, *supra* note 13.

Table 2-2 Bull and Bear Markets[30] (S&P 500 Index*)

Bull or Bear?	Start Date	End Date	Months	Change	Bull or Bear?	Start Date	End Date	Months	Change
Bull	08/01/1921	09/07/1929	97.3	395%	Bull	10/07/1966	11/29/1968	25.8	48%
Bear	09/07/1929	06/01/1932	32.8	−86%	Bear	11/29/1968	05/26/1970	17.9	−36%
Bull	06/01/1932	07/18/1933	13.5	177%	Bull	05/26/1970	01/11/1973	31.6	74%
Bear	07/18/1933	03/14/1935	19.9	−34%	Bear	01/11/1973	10/03/1974	20.7	−48%
Bull	03/14/1935	03/06/1937	23.8	132%	Bull	10/03/1974	11/28/1980	73.9	126%
Bear	03/06/1937	03/31/1938	12.8	−55%	Bear	11/28/1980	08/12/1982	20.4	−27%
Bull	03/31/1938	11/09/1938	7.3	62%	Bull	08/12/1982	08/25/1987	60.4	229%
Bear	11/09/1938	04/28/1942	41.6	−46%	Bear	08/25/1987	12/04/1987	3.3	−34%
Bull	04/28/1942	05/29/1946	49	158%	Bull	12/04/1987	07/16/1990	31.4	65%
Bear	05/29/1946	05/17/1947	11.6	−28%	Bear	07/16/1990	10/11/1990	2.9	−20%
Bull	05/17/1947	06/15/1948	13	22%	Bull	10/11/1990	03/24/2000	113.4	417%
Bear	06/15/1948	06/13/1949	11.9	−21%	Bear	03/24/2000	10/09/2002	30.5	−49%
Bull	06/13/1949	08/02/1956	85.7	267%	Bull	10/09/2002	10/09/2007	60	101%
Bear	08/02/1956	10/22/1957	14.7	−22%	Bear	10/09/2007	03/09/2009	17	−57%
Bull	10/22/1957	12/12/1961	49.7	86%	Bull	03/09/2009	02/19/2020	131.5	401%
Bear	12/12/1961	06/26/1962	6.4	−28%	Bear	02/19/2020	03/23/2020	1.1	−34%
Bull	06/26/1962	02/09/1966	43.5	80%	Bull	03/23/2020	12/31/2020	8.6	68%

Source: Sam Stovall, Chief Investment Strategist, CFRA Research
*See Note to Table 2-2.

Note: The S&P 500 Index tracks large-capitalization (large-cap) stocks. The S&P 500 Index was introduced in 1957; data shown as S&P 500 Index for years before 1957 uses other large-cap indices or measures, such as the S&P Composite Index. S&P Global describes the history: "In 1923, in an effort to reflect market trends, the Standard Statistics Company developed its first stock index. This precursor of the S&P 500 tracked 233 U.S. stocks and was calculated weekly. In 1926, it was reformulated as the Composite Stock Index, which tracked 90 stocks and was calculated daily. Over time, the number of securities grew and the frequency of calculation increased until, in March 1957, the S&P 500 debuted in the format that persists today."[31]

---

30. *Id.*
31. https://www.spglobal.com/spdji/en/research-insights/index-literacy/the-sp-500 -and-the-dow/.

During a vicious bear market, you'll see dramatic daily price declines. Table 2-3 illustrates the drama we experienced during the coronavirus and earlier markets. Note that the third largest daily loss occurred on March 16, 2020 (-12.0 percent), just shy of October 28, 1929's loss of 12.3 percent. The coronavirus market accounted for three of the largest 25 daily losses. The Financial Crisis (2008) accounted for four of the 25 largest daily losses. Thirteen out of 25 largest losses were in the 1920s (the stock market peaked in August 1929) and 1930s.

Table 2-3 Largest Daily Losses (S&P 500 Index*)

Rank	Date	Change	Rank	Date	Change
1	10/19/1987	−20.5%	13	10/26/1987	−8.3%
2	10/28/1929	−12.3%	14	10/05/1932	−8.2%
3	03/16/2020	−12.0%	15	08/12/1932	−8.0%
4	10/29/1929	−10.2%	16	05/31/1932	−7.8%
5	11/06/1929	−9.9%	17	07/26/1934	−7.8%
6	03/12/2020	−9.5%	18	10/09/2008	−7.6%
7	10/18/1937	−9.3%	19	03/09/2020	−7.6%
8	10/15/2008	−9.0%	20	05/14/1940	−7.5%
9	12/01/2008	−8.9%	21	09/24/1931	−7.3%
10	07/20/1933	−8.9%	22	09/12/1932	−7.2%
11	09/29/2008	−8.8%	23	06/15/1933	−7.0%
12	07/21/1933	−8.7%	24	10/27/1997	−6.9%
			25	08/31/1998	−6.8%

Source: Sam Stovall, Chief Investment Strategist, CFRA Research
*See Note to Table 2-2.

Bear markets' daily volatility swings upward, not just downward, as you can see from the next table showing largest daily gains. Two of the largest daily gains were clocked during the coronavirus bear market (March 13, 2020, and March 24, 2020). March 23, 2020 marked the bottom of the coronavirus bear.

The Financial Crisis accounted for two of the 25 largest daily gains (the Financial Crisis bear market ended in March 2009), as shown in Table 2-4. Nineteen out of twenty-five of the largest daily gains were in the 1920s and 1930s.

Table 2-4 Largest Daily Gains (S&P 500 Index*)

Rank	Date	Change	Rank	Date	Change
1	03/15/1933	16.6%	13	08/03/1932	8.9%
2	10/30/1929	12.5%	14	10/08/1931	8.6%
3	10/06/1931	12.4%	15	02/13/1932	8.4%
4	09/21/1932	11.8%	16	12/18/1931	8.3%
5	10/13/2008	11.6%	17	02/11/1932	8.3%
6	10/28/2008	10.8%	18	07/24/1933	8.1%
7	09/05/1939	9.6%	19	06/10/1932	7.7%
8	04/20/1933	9.5%	20	06/03/1931	7.5%
9	3/24/2020	9.4%	21	05/15/1948	7.5%
10	3/13/2020	9.3%	22	11/10/1932	7.5%
11	10/21/1987	9.1%	23	10/20/1937	7.5%
12	11/14/1929	9.0%	24	06/19/1933	7.2%
			25	05/06/1932	7.2%

Source: Sam Stovall, Chief Investment Strategist, CFRA Research
*See Note to Table 2-2.

Next, let's consider stock market returns from year to year and within a year. This data is essential in providing additional perspective on how the stock market functions.

Intra-Year Volatility

Novices can fail to appreciate that even up years suffer pullbacks during the year. For example, 1980 ended with a return of over 26 percent after declining by 17 percent during the year.[32] (The 17 percent figure is an "intra-year" decline, measured from a mid-year peak to trough, instead of the beginning of a calendar year.) This is an important data point that needs to be understood—particularly by retirees, as retirees can be more sensitive than young investors to declines in the value of their investments.

---

32. Data from *Guide to to the Markets*, J.P. Morgan Asset Management, 16 (2021), https://am.jpmorgan.com/content/dam/jpm-am-aem/global/en/insights/market-insights /guide-to-the-markets/mi-guide-to-the-markets-us.pdf

For that reason, this piece of market knowledge is probably more important to understand than just about any other, since mistakes are made
when fear directs action.

Figure 2-1 shows the intra-year declines versus calendar-year returns
for the S&P 500 Index for select years.[33] Table 2-5 shows calendar-year
returns and intra-year declines for each year from 1980 through 2020.

**Figure 2-1 Intra-Year Declines versus Calendar-Year Returns, 1980–2020
(S&P 500 Index*)**

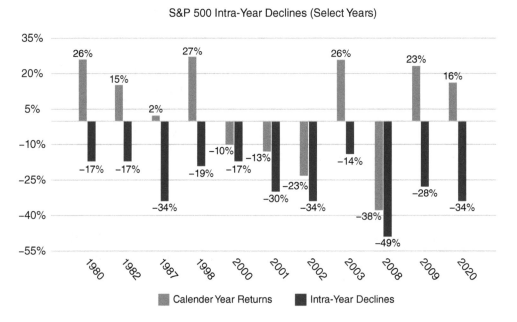

S&P 500 Intra-Year Declines (Select Years)

*Look at note 32 for guidance.

From 1980 through 2020, about 20 percent (nine out of 41 years)
ended with declines for the year, as can be seen from Table 2-5. However, short-term intra-year declines occurred 100 percent of the time,
even when the year ended with a positive return. These short-term
movements can spook a novice investor out of the market at the wrong
time. The challenge for the retiree is to maintain perspective as markets move—perspective based on knowledge—as well as the discipline
to follow a strategy set out for the management of the retirement portfolio, the subject of Part II of this book.

---

33. *Id.*

Table 2-5 Intra-Year Declines 1980–2020 (S&P 500 Index)

Year	Calendar Return	Intra-Year Declines	Year	Calendar Return	Intra-Year Declines
1980	26%	–17%	2000	–10%	–17%
1981	–10%	–18%	2001	–13%	–30%
1982	15%	–17%	2002	–23%	–34%
1983	17%	–7%	2003	26%	–14%
1984	1%	–13%	2004	9%	–8%
1985	26%	–8%	2005	3%	–7%
1986	15%	–9%	2006	14%	–8%
1987	2%	–34%	2007	4%	–10%
1988	12%	–8%	2008	–38%	–49%
1989	27%	–8%	2009	23%	–28%
1990	–7%	–20%	2010	13%	–16%
1991	26%	–6%	2011	0%	–19%
1992	4%	–6%	2012	13%	–10%
1993	7%	–5%	2013	30%	–6%
1994	–2%	–9%	2014	11%	–7%
1995	34%	–3%	2015	–1%	–12%
1996	20%	–8%	2016	10%	–11%
1997	31%	–11%	2017	19%	–3%
1998	27%	–19%	2018	–6%	–20%
1999	20%	–12%	2019	29%	–7%
			2020	16%	–34%

Data from J.P. Morgan Asset Management[34]

Time Diversification

When viewed over long horizons, decades long, the significance of intra-year and year-over-year volatility takes on a different meaning. Viewed in hindsight with the perspective of decades instead of days, volatility "diminishes" as holding periods lengthen. Figure 2-2 illustrates this phenomenon, known as "time diversification."

---

34. *Id.*

For example, the widest divergence occurred during the shortest period as shown in the far-left portion of Figure 2-2. Returns ranged between a high (54.4 percent) and a low (–43.5 percent) during one-year holding periods. On the far right you can see that 40-year holding periods had a much narrower range, from a high of 12.5 percent to a low of 8.8 percent. Twenty-year holding periods ranged from a high of 17.9 percent to a low of 3.1 percent.

Figure 2-2 Best, Median, and Worst Annualized Returns for One-Time Investment in S&P 500 Index Fund* with Dividends Reinvested for Rolling Holding Periods from 1927 through 2020

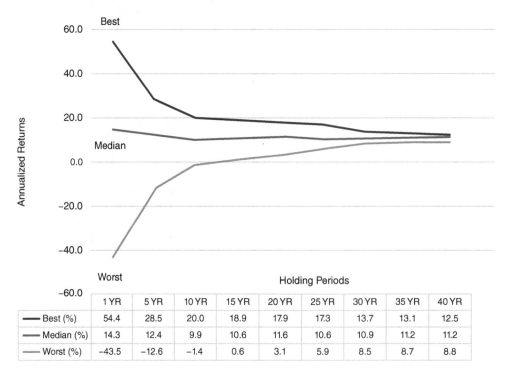

	1 YR	5 YR	10 YR	15 YR	20 YR	25 YR	30 YR	35 YR	40 YR
—— Best (%)	54.4	28.5	20.0	18.9	17.9	17.3	13.7	13.1	12.5
—— Median (%)	14.3	12.4	9.9	10.6	11.6	10.6	10.9	11.2	11.2
—— Worst (%)	–43.5	–12.6	–1.4	0.6	3.1	5.9	8.5	8.7	8.8

Source: Jackson, Grant.[35]

*See Note to Table 2-2. Also note that we are using the S&P 500 Index as a proxy (before fees and expenses) for an S&P 500 Index Fund investment.

---

35. S&P 500 Index return data in the chart is provided by the Capital Group Hypothetical Tool. Capital Group is one of the world's largest investment managers and home to the American Funds.

What does this data mean to you as a present or future retiree? Your holding period will extend from the time you construct your retirement portfolio until you pass away, and longer if there is legacy intent. Say that horizon is 20 years or longer. During that holding period, looking back, your properly structured portfolio will have ridden out interim turbulence.

Key Takeaways

This chapter's review of historical market returns can help the discerning investor get some context before taking action. With this data, you can envision how a plan might develop that avoids reacting to interim market moves. The goal is to plan ahead, not to react.

As a discerning investor, consider the following:

- Avoid the understandable temptation to flee the stock market during downward price movements, unless you are investing without a plan. Daily and intra-year volatility are realities for every investor.
- If you sell at the wrong time, such as a market bottom, you will lock in a loss and potentially prevent a recovery unless you re-enter the market at the right time. Getting out is easy; when do you get back in?
- Maintain perspective as markets move. Short-term volatility becomes manageable to the discerning investor.

In general, you want to set your strategy for the long-term. That's the rule for the retirement investor who wants to secure decades of the retirement timeline, but that also assumes that the retiree is managing his or her portfolio properly to account for and manage risk, which we will address next.

Note that the next two chapters (3 and 4) provide additional context on how to think of the financial markets. This is information that will be most interesting to self-directed investors and those who want an understanding of some of the underlying theories that guide professionals.

Chapter 3
Uncertainty: The Investor's Dilemma

The dilemma all investors face is the natural desire to want great certainty of achieving high returns. The markets don't work that way.

In this chapter, let's continue the volatility and risk dialogue we started in the last chapter by expanding the discussion beyond the stock market. This chapter will help you prepare for the risk and volatility that is inevitably part of investing for retirement.

I'll share just a few of the valuable insights of Nobel Prize–winning economist Harry Markowitz, who created the foundation of modern portfolio theory (MPT). I'll also show you a very simple example of how an individual investor can put MPT's risk and reward concepts to use.

Only the Clairvoyant Can Predict the Market with Certainty

First, some context: Markowitz posited the investor's dilemma—wanting a return that was both high and certain (risk-free)—in *Portfolio Selection: Efficient Diversification of Investments*.[1] Originally published as his doctoral thesis in 1952, Markowitz's work helps quantify risk and return expectations for investors.

According to Markowitz:

Uncertainty is a salient feature of security investment. Economic forces are not understood well enough for predictions to be beyond doubt or error. Even if the consequences of economic conditions were understood perfectly, noneconomic influences can change the course of general prosperity, the level of the market, or

---

1. Harry M. Markowitz, Portfolio Selection: Efficient Diversification of Investments 6 (Yale Univ. Press 1959/1970). You can download a copy of the work at m16-all.pdf.

the success of a particular security. . . . We are expecting too much if we require the security analyst to predict with certainty whether a typical security will increase or decrease in value. . . . *Only the clairvoyant could hope to predict with certainty.*[2]

Markowitz's points are well taken. Expect uncertainty in the markets. Also expect that analysts cannot predict the direction of the markets nor the price of a security with certainty. Even when all possible considerations are factored into the equation, they can change instantly. Even those who consult a crystal ball can only *hope* to predict the future.

This is the rule to live by: uncertainty has to be accepted as part of the investment equation, and, further, uncertainty needs to be weighed against likely return.

In Markowitz's words:

The most reliable portfolio with an extremely high likely return may be subject to an *unacceptably high degree of uncertainty.* The portfolio with the least uncertainty may have an undesirably small "likely return."[3]

Again, these points are well taken, insightful, and extremely helpful to any investor, but especially a retiree. An aggressive investor can live with a higher degree of uncertainty, which is the price he must be willing to pay for a potentially higher return. A more conservative investor (a retiree) striving for retirement security, would be less willing to do so.

In my experience, the most satisfied investors are those who embrace the investor's dilemma, understanding that risk (uncertainty) and reward (high returns) are forever and always intertwined. These discerning investors focus on managing their portfolios to achieve their own personal objectives, while managing risk and tempering expectations to what the markets can reasonably provide.

How can you follow in their footsteps? First, you will need a foundation. What do the experts say about structuring portfolios that could be useful? How would you attempt to structure a personal portfolio that has a good risk-return profile?

---

2. *Id.* at 4 (emphasis added).
3. *Id.* at 6 (emphasis added).

How to Lessen Risk with Diversification

To minimize risk, you want the portfolio to contain assets that are not all going to act the same way at the same time. Part of the exercise is to review each holding's risk and reward parameters to see how holdings correlate with each other. The bond market, for example, does not normally track the stock market.

If a portfolio holds assets that are noncorrelated, the portfolio is said to be "diversified." (Assets that are "noncorrelated" wouldn't react to market-moving events in tandem, whereas correlated assets would.)

According to Markowitz:

> The correlation among returns is *not* the same for all securities. We generally expect the returns on a security to be more correlated with those in the same industry than those of unrelated industries. . . . To reduce risk, it is necessary to avoid a portfolio whose securities are all highly correlated with each other. One hundred securities whose returns rise and fall in near unison afford little more protection than the uncertain return of a single security.[4]

Diversified Portfolios: Risk Free?

Markowitz cautions that "diversification can reduce risk but not eliminate it."[5] This statement is noteworthy. The principles of diversification do not guarantee against losses. Even a well-diversified portfolio will suffer when the entire financial system is threatened with collapse, as during the 2007–2009 Financial Crisis.

Asset Class Returns over the Long Term

Historically, a diversified portfolio of large company stocks represented by the S&P 500 Index offered returns of about 10 percent per year on average (1926 through 2020).[6] That 10 percent figure is "total return,"

---

4. *Id.* at 5 (emphasis added).
5. *Id.*
6. Roger G. Ibbotson, 2021 SBBI® Yearbook Stocks, Bonds, Bills, and Inflation: U.S. Capital Markets Performance by Asset Class 1926–2020, at 4-5 (Duff & Phelps 2021). This is a nominal return, meaning before inflation. If inflation is factored in, the annualized "real" return is 7.2 percent. Also, see Note to Table 2-2.

which includes capital appreciation plus dividends. For example, in 2009, the total return was 26.5 percent (capital appreciation of 23.5 percent plus dividend yield of 3.0 percent).[7] In 2018, the S&P 500 Index was down 4.4 percent (capital depreciation of –6.2 percent plus dividend yield of 1.8 percent).[8] Annual swings for the same period (1926 through 2020) ranged from a high of 54.0 percent in 1933 to a low of –43.5 percent in 1931.[9]

Table 3-1[10] incorporates the bull and bear markets we discussed in Chapter 2 (see large cap stocks (representing S&P 500 Index) organized by highest to lowest returns). The table also shows standard deviation, which measures volatility, a topic we will review in the next chapter. Briefly, the higher the standard deviation, the greater the volatility.

Table 3-1 Asset Classes, Returns and Standard Deviation (1926–2020)

	Average Annual Total Returns	Standard Deviation	$1 invested 12/31/1925 held through 12/31/2020
Small-cap Stocks	11.9%	31.3%	$41,978
Large-cap Stocks	10.3%	19.7%	$10,945
Long-term Corporate Bonds	6.2%	8.5%	$297
Long-term Government Bonds	5.7%	9.8%	$186
Intermediate-term Government Bonds	5.1%	5.6%	$115
U.S. Treasury Bills	3.3%	3.1%	$22
Inflation	2.9%	4.0%	$15

Data from 2021 SBBI[11]

---

7. *Id.* at 2-9, Exhibit 2.4.

8. Roger G. Ibbotson, 2020 SBBI® Yearbook Stocks, Bonds, Bills, and Inflation: U.S. Capital Markets Performance by Asset Class 1926–2020, at 2-9. Exhibit 2.4 (Duff & Phelps 2021).

9. *Id.* at 2-8, Appendices A-1 through A-3.

10. *Id.* at 2-2, Exhibit 2.1.

11. Ibbotson, *supra* note 6, at 2-6 and 3-1. Ibbotson defines the asset classes listed in Table 3-1 as follows: Small-cap stocks are 9th and 10th decile market capitalization stocks. Large-cap stocks are based on the S&P 500 Index (before 1957, 90 of the largest stocks). Long-term corporate bonds are represented by the FTSE US BIG Corp AAA/AA 10+ Yr. Long-term government bonds have maturities of 20 years. Intermediate-term government bonds have maturities of five years. U.S. Treasury Bills have maturities of one month or the shortest period available after one month. Ibbotson uses the Consumer

As you can see from Table 3-1, small-cap stocks exhibited the highest total return and the highest standard deviation, indicating a wild ride, and an exceptional outcome for the period from 1926 through 2020. Be careful of drawing conclusions about what to invest in based on this data. We need to understand the trade-off between risk and reward first, the subject of this and later chapters.

At this point, let's return to the question of how an individual could benefit from the concepts we've discussed so far in this chapter.

Practical Application Example

If I told you that a retirement portfolio benefits from diversification by sector and asset class, would you agree? Doubters might ask: why not just buy an S&P 500 Index Fund to avoid the work that goes into structuring and managing a portfolio?

Note: For purposes of return calculations using hypothetical software, we are using the S&P 500 Index as a proxy (before fees and expenses) for an S&P 500 Index Fund investment. For this discussion, income taxes are addressed in Appendix A.

Perfect Timing: When the Market Was a "Sure Bet"

To fully appreciate risk and reward, we have to time the investment to your retirement date. Why not pick a perfect time, when the market appears to you to be a sure bet. Such a time was 1999, when newspapers were reporting that new technology (the Internet) had changed the rules of investing.[12] The stock market was only going up. (Of course, hindsight proved otherwise.)

I'll show you three periods: "A" assumes retiring at the end of 1999, the top of the market, through 2002, the bottom of the market. "B" assumes retiring at the end of period A. "C" extends A to pick up retiring at the

---

Price Index for All Urban Consumers (CPI-U), not seasonally adjusted, as its source for measuring inflation. The CPI began series data in 1913.

12. E.S. Browning, *Stocks Approach the Stratosphere*, WALL ST. J. (Jan. 3, 2000, 11:59 PM), https://www.wsj.com/articles/SB945191069234483337.

end of 1999 through 2020. In each case, we're just buying and holding an S&P 500 Index Fund and comparing it to a large, well-known balanced fund (stocks and bonds) with a long history of good performance (the fund is labeled "Balanced Fund" in the discussion that follows).[13] In the footnotes, you'll also find average total returns for the 40 largest balanced funds.[14] The purpose of comparing a balanced fund to an S&P 500 fund is to see how a less-volatile balanced fund acted during this declining market period, compared to an up market.

Later in the chapter we'll return to these three periods and add the effect of withdrawals. *In all instances, the S&P 500 Index serves as a proxy (before fees and expenses) for an S&P Index Fund investment.*

Period A: Start at a Market Top (1999–2002)

You invested $1 million in an S&P 500 Index Fund at the end of 1999, which you *later* discovered was the top of a very long 113-month bull market that extended from 10/11/1990 to 3/24/2000 and returned 417 percent. Instead of being a good time to invest your retirement savings, over the next three years, you saw declines of –9.1 percent in 2000, –11.9 percent in 2001, and –22.1 percent in 2002. By then, your $1 million had declined to about $624,000. See Table 3-2.

Table 3-2 12/31/1999 to 12/31/2002[15]

Funds	12/31/2002 Value ($1 million invested)	Annualized Total Returns 12/31/1999–12/31/2002
Balanced Fund[16]	$1,174,845	5.5%
S&P 500 Index Fund	$624,064	–14.5%

---

13. The "Balanced Fund" is categorized in the "balanced" objective grouping and the "allocation" category group by Morningstar, with an equity allocation of 50 percent to 70 percent. The manager is Capital Group.

14. For a frame of reference, I've also included returns for the largest 40 similarly categorized balanced funds including the balanced fund in the tables. (Referred to as the "*Balanced Average*" in subsequent footnotes.) The average is calculated using Morningstar® Advisor Workstation[SM].

15. Data sourced from Capital Group Hypothetical Tool sourced from Refinitiv, which is one of the world's largest providers of financial markets data. Capital Group is one of the world's largest investment managers, sponsor of the American Funds.

16. The *Balanced Average supra* note 14 ended with $924,741, with a loss of 2.6 percent for the period 12/31/1999 to 12/31/2002.

During the same period (12/31/1999 to 12/31/2002), the Balanced Fund[17] grew to about $1.2 million. The Balance Fund's returns were: up 15.9 percent in 2000; up 8.2 percent in 2001; and down 6.3 percent in 2002, in contrast to the S&P 500 Fund's three down years.

This experience shows the benefits of diversification (in this case, adding bonds); you cannot predict when a booming stock market will quickly turn into a bear.

Now, let's look at starting a retirement portfolio at a market bottom.

Period B: Start at a Market Bottom (2002–2020)

What if you had retired at the end of 2002, which no one knew was the bottom at the time? Diversification with bonds would have led to underperformance compared to the S&P 500 Index Fund.

The S&P 500 Index Fund, being more volatile and investing solely in stocks, outperformed the Balanced Fund in the upturn (12/31/2002 to 12/31/2020) by far, even though this period included the Financial Crisis and the coronavirus market (10.6 percent for the S&P 500 Index Fund versus 8.6 percent for the Balanced Fund).[18] During that time frame, the S&P 500 Index Fund's 2020 ending value was $6.1 million on $1 million invested 12/31/2002, compared to $4.4 million for the Balanced Fund, as shown in Table 3-3.

Table 3-3 12/31/2002 to 12/31/2020[19]

Funds	12/31/2020 Value ($1 million invested)	Annualized Total Returns 12/31/2002–12/31/2020
Balanced Fund[20]	$4,417,804	8.6%
S&P 500 Index Fund	$6,118,516	10.6%

Let's go back and pick up the entire period from 1999 to 2020.

---

17. Assume a $1 million investment in the Balanced Fund and a $1 million investment in the S&P 500 Index Fund with dividends reinvested from 12/31/1999 through 12/31/2002.

18. Assume a $1 million investment in the Balanced Fund and a $1 million investment in the S&P 500 Index Fund with dividends reinvested from 12/31/2002 through 12/31/2020.

19. Data sourced from Capital Group Hypothetical Tool.

20. The *Balanced Average supra* note 14 ended with $4 million with a return of 8.1 percent for the period 12/31/2002 to 12/31/2020. Morningstar® Advisor Workstation[SM].

Period C: Start at Period A and Hold through Period B (1999–2020)

How did diversification work for the longer period, assuming the 1999 retiree was still invested (from 12/31/1999 to 12/31/2020)? For this longer period, the Balanced Fund outperformed (8.2 percent for the Balanced Fund versus 6.6 percent for the S&P 500 Index Fund).[21] The S&P 500 Index Fund's ending 2020 value was $3.8 million on the original 12/31/1999 $1 million investment, compared to $5.2 million for the Balanced Fund, as shown in Table 3-4.

Part of the reason for the Balanced Fund's long-term outperformance is the period we're looking at—during the down markets, the Balanced Fund lost less than the S&P 500 Fund. The largest drawdown during the period was greater for the S&P 500 Fund (51.0 percent peak to trough decline) than the Balanced Fund (36.9 percent).[22] This is a very important point to understand for the retiree whose investment horizon is decades long.

Table 3-4 12/31/1999 to 12/31/2020[23]

Funds	12/31/2020 Value ($1 million invested)	Annualized Total Returns 12/31/1999–12/31/2020
Balanced Fund[24]	$5,190,236	8.2%
S&P 500 Index Fund	$3,818,347	6.6%

What can you take away from looking at these three periods? Are there benefits of investing less aggressively for time horizons that include both bulls and bears? Are these the types of markets that retirees will likely face, due to the length of retirement?

---

21. Assume a $1 million investment in the Balanced Fund and a $1 million investment in the S&P 500 Index Fund with dividends reinvested from 12/31/1999 through 12/31/2020.

22. Reports, graphs, analysis, and data generated with STEELE Mutual Fund Expert Software, www.MutualFundExpert.com. Copyright © Steele Systems, Inc. 2020. All rights reserved.

23. Data sourced from Capital Group Hypothetical Tool.

24. The *Balanced Average supra* note 14 ended with $3.75 million, with a return of 6.5 percent for the period 12/31/1999 to 12/31/2020. Morningstar® Advisor Workstation[SM].

Sequence of Return Risk: Portfolio Withdrawals

As you saw from the discussion, the market you retire into will determine your results. In the discussion, we did not include the effect of taking withdrawals to pay for living expenses. Let's do that now.

When you start to use your portfolio to cover living expenses, you can do serious damage by retiring at the wrong time, that is, at the top of the market. This is called sequence of return risk. Having to take out money in a down year has a much larger consequence at the beginning of retirement than in the middle or the end of retirement. According to the CFA Institute, "Numerous studies have shown that poor returns in the early phases of decumulation have a more damaging effect on retirement income than poor returns that come later."[25]

First, let's focus on a single holding, looking at different market periods from the 1920s, to see the impact of withdrawals.

Figure 3-1 shows the median and worst 30-year rolling periods in the market from 1928 through 2020. Each scenario assumes $1 million invested at retirement in an S&P 500 Index Fund* with dividends reinvested, with 4 percent annual withdrawals ($40,000) increasing by 3 percent per year, *without tax considerations.* (*See Note to Table 2-2.)

Note: Hypotheticals calculate returns for $1 million invested in an S&P 500 Index (as if the index were a fund) with dividends reinvested, over 30-year rolling periods, beginning 12/31/1927 and ending 12/31/2020. Withdrawals are $40,000 in the first year and increase by 3 percent annually. The portfolio values on the y-axis are in a logarithmic scale (in this case multiples of 10); the portfolio values are shown this way to better illustrate the range of possible outcomes. (See Note to Table 2-2.)

---

25. Keyur Patel, *Managing Sequence Risk to Optimize Retirement Income.* Financial Analysts Journal Abstract, Fourth Quarter 2017, https://www.cfainstitute.org/research/financial-analysts-journal/2017/managing-sequence-risk.

Figure 3-1 Sequence of Return Risk of the S&P 500 Index* Median and Worst Performing 30-Year Rolling Periods from 1928 to 2020

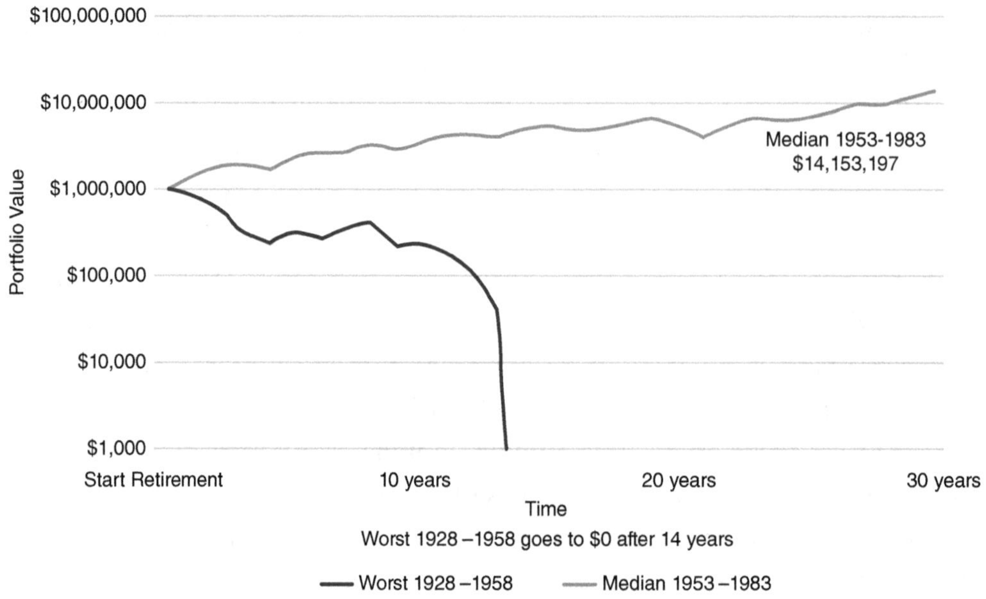

Worst 1928 –1958 goes to $0 after 14 years

— Worst 1928 –1958   — Median 1953 –1983

Source: Jackson, Grant. Data from Capital Group Hypothetical Tool.

*See Note to Table 2-2.

The median (1953–1983) scenario finished 30 years with $14 million remaining. The worst scenario (1928–1958) starts off with one of the worst decades in the market and runs out of money after 14 years. It's that worst case scenario that needs to be avoided, and it does not show the impact of taxes, which would further exacerbate the situation.

Let's incorporate withdrawals into the examples we reviewed together earlier in this chapter for the same three time periods. Let's withdraw 4 percent per year to spend, increasing the withdrawal by 3 percent yearly to account for inflation. We'll incorporate taxes in Appendix A.

Period A: Start at a Market Top (1999–2002)

As shown in Table 3-5, for the period 12/31/1999 to 12/31/2002, withdrawals came to $123,636. Ending values were $1,048,400 for the Balanced Fund and $528,385 for the S&P 500 Fund.

Table 3-5 (12/31/1999 to 12/31/2002) 4 Percent Withdrawals + 3 Percent Annual Increases

Funds	12/31/2002 Value ($1 million invested)	Annualized Total Returns 12/31/1999–12/31/2002	Total Withdrawals
Balanced Fund[26]	$1,048,400	5.8%	$123,636
S&P 500 Index Fund	$528,385	–14.4%	$123,636

Withdrawals are made monthly on the last day of the month.[27]

Let's turn to starting at a market bottom.

Period B: Start at a Market Bottom (2002–2020)

Table 3-6 shows the second period we reviewed earlier (12/31/2002 to 12/31/2020). Withdrawals totaled $936,577. Ending values were $2,317,989 for the Balanced Fund and $3,379,378 for the S&P 500 Index Fund.

Table 3-6 (12/31/2002 to 12/31/2020) 4 Percent Withdrawals + 3 Percent Annual Increases

Funds	12/31/2020 Value ($1 million invested)	Annualized Total Returns 12/31/2002–12/31/2020	Total Withdrawals
Balanced Fund[28]	$2,317,989	8.4%	$936,577
S&P 500 Index Fund	$3,379,378	10.2%	$936,577

Withdrawals are made monthly on the last day of the month.[29]

Period C: Start at Period A and Hold through Period B (1999–2020)

The third period includes periods A and B (12/31/1999 to 12/31/2020), as shown in Table 3-7. Withdrawals totaled $1,147,059. Ending values were $2,162,892 for the Balanced Fund and $205,698 for the S&P 500 Index Fund.

---

26. The *Balanced Average supra* note 14 ended with $810,778 for a loss of –2.4 percent for the period 12/31/1999 to 12/31/2002. Morningstar® Advisor Workstation[SM].
27. Data sourced from Capital Group Hypothetical Tool.
28. The *Balanced Average supra* note 14 ended with $2.1 million, with a return of 8.0 percent for the period 12/31/2002 to 12/31/2020. Morningstar® Advisor Workstation[SM].
29. Data sourced from Capital Group Hypothetical Tool.

Table 3-7 (12/31/1999 to 12/31/2020) 4 Percent Withdrawals + 3 Percent Annual Increases

Funds	12/31/2020 Value ($1 million invested)	Annualized Total Returns 12/31/1999–12/31/2020	Total Withdrawals
Balanced Fund[30]	$2,261,852	7.8%	$1,147,059
S&P 500 Index Fund	$205,698	2.4%	$1,147,059

Withdrawals are made monthly on the last day of the month.[31]

Note: Tables 3-1 through 3-7 assume a tax-deferred or tax-free (Roth) experience. What if the accounts were taxable? Turn to Appendix A for a before- and after-tax comparison of Table 3-7.

The bottom line is this: Anyone embarking on retirement needs to factor in the potential for great harm if sequence risk isn't taken into account, together with an appreciation for the benefits of incorporating bonds into the equation. The fact is that you don't know what type of market you'll retire into.

During the construction phase of a retirement portfolio, that is, when the portfolio is being organized, it's wise to consider the effect of a potential downturn at the start of retirement. Without going into details here, you would do this by setting an appropriately diversified portfolio strategy that is built around your capital, cash flow needs, and time horizon, subjects we'll discuss more fully in Part II of the book.

Obvious Risk: A Wet Hand; an Electrical Socket

The importance of managing risks (whether they are obvious or not) cannot be overestimated. As the authors of *Risk Management: An Introduction* stated:

---

30. The *Balanced Average supra* note 14 ended with $1.14 million, with a return of 5.6 percent for the period 12/31/1999 to 12/31/2020. Morningstar® Advisor Workstation[SM].

31. Data sourced from Capital Group Hypothetical Tool (and Morningstar® Advisor Workstation[SM] for after-tax consistency in Appendix A).

Although many individuals do take reasonable precautions against unwanted risks, these precautions are often against *obvious* risks, such as *sticking a wet hand into an electrical socket or swallowing poison.* The more *subtle* risks are often ignored. Many individuals simply do not view risk management as a formal, systematic process that would help them achieve not only their financial goals, but also the ultimate end result of happiness, or maximum utility as economists like to call it, but they should.[32]

Identifying sources of risk, both obvious and subtle, will need to be an ongoing part of your portfolio construction and review process.

In my experience, the ideal retirement portfolio marries uncertainty and potential return in such a way that the retiree is comfortable with risk and reward trade-offs. This helps the portfolio manager structure a portfolio that has return potential that can meet the long-term needs of the retiree in spite of the types of intra-year and bear market moves that will inevitably be part of the retiree's investment horizon.

Key Takeaways

Uncertainty is part of an investor's life. By definition, an investment involves an assessment of—some would say "a bet" on—the future. The purchase of a stock is made in anticipation of a profit on the sale of the stock and in some cases, dividends along the way. The purchase of a bond anticipates interest payments until maturity (along with price changes as interest rates change during the holding period). But neither can be certain.

The discerning investor understands that risk is imbedded in every investment and that upside reward is the desired prize but not a given.

- While you can choose when you will retire, you cannot choose the market you will experience. Sequence risk is real and caution needs to be paramount when planning ahead.
- Remember that every investment has its own risks. Be wary of investment offerings that downplay risk or exaggerate reward.

---

32. Don M. Chance, PhD, CFA, & Michael E. Edleson, PhD, CFA, Risk Management: An Introduction (CFA Institute 2015) (emphasis added).

- Diversification (using a collection of assets that are not correlated to each other) can help achieve "better" returns over time periods that include market declines. However, diversification does not eliminate risk.
- Consider whether you will be pulled into taking more risk than appropriate when the market is on an extended upswing—*when bull markets run.*

We'll take a closer look at risk measurement in the next chapter.

Chapter 4
Measures for the Risk-Averse Investor

In the last chapter, we looked at how to think of risk based on uncertainty and managing the variability of returns. In this chapter, we'll take the discussion further, to enable you to see how a financial firm might measure risk. We'll discuss academic theories and practical applications, ending with a short illustration of how to take advantage of risk measures.

This discussion will enable you to better understand the trade-off between risk and reward and help lead to potentially more effective decisions—a bonus when moving into retirement.

Setting the Stage

Before Modern Portfolio Theory (MPT) incorporated risk versus return concepts, investments were chosen based on expected returns.[1] In 1952, MPT introduced the insight that there is a trade-off between risk and reward, a very useful concept for any investor who is comparing one investment to another. MPT measures risk using standard deviation of returns, which captures both positive and negative returns around the "average."[2] Standard deviation assumes that upside and downside risks are symmetrical.

But, isn't the risk-averse investor more concerned about the downward movements? Shouldn't risk measurement be asymmetrical, to isolate the downside? So concluded Frank Sortino, a professor of finance at

---

1. Modern Portfolio Theory was advanced in Harry Markowitz, Portfolio Selection: Efficient Diversification of Investments 6 (Yale Univ. Press 1959/1970). You can download a copy of the work at m16-all.pdf.

2. For example, if the average return is 5 percent and the standard deviation is 10 percent, you are just as likely to gain 15 percent (5 percent plus 10 percent) as you are to lose 5 percent (5 percent minus 10 percent).

San Francisco State University in the 1980s. He introduced the concept of Post-Modern Portfolio Theory,[3] or PMPT, measuring downside deviation. Standard deviation and downside deviation are both used to understand the historical volatility of investments. Later in this chapter, we will look at an illustration of these and other risk measures.

Standard deviation assumes that upside and downside risks are symmetrical; in contrast, downside deviation focuses only on the downside.

MPT's Efficient Frontier

To judge the volatility of a selection of holdings using MPT, one can plot a graph representing an array with different risk and reward characteristics (see Figure 4-1). Markowitz terms this type of graph the "efficient frontier." Think of the efficient frontier as a way to compare a number of investments or portfolios to plot return against risk, the best option being the investments that offer the highest return for the risk assumed.

The graph illustrates portfolio return and risk ranging from 100 percent U.S. intermediate government bonds to 100 percent U.S. large cap stocks.[4]

You can use an efficient frontier graph to help align your portfolio to your risk appetite. For example, an investor who is *most concerned about volatility* might want to position his or her portfolio in the lower left portion of the graph (low standard deviation), as long as he or she is willing to accept lower returns. In contrast, an investor who is *most concerned about potential returns* (and accepting of volatility) might choose the upper right portion of the graph.[5] A discerning investor who needs to support him or herself in retirement might take the middle ground after determining cash flow generation (discussed in Part II of the book).

---

3. In 1996, Sortino together with Hal Forsey, also a professor at San Francisco State University, wrote *On the Use and Misuse of Downside Risk*. Later, Brian Rom and Kathleen Ferguson from Investment Technologies worked with Sortino to develop commercial applications of Post-Modern Portfolio Theory.

4. Data sourced from 2020 SBBI® Yearbook Stocks, Bonds, Bills, and Inflation. Accessed through CFA Institute website, www.cfainstitute.org.

5. For the curious, using a combination of a risk-free asset (T-bills) and the highest Sharpe ratio portfolio can create portfolios outside of the efficient frontier; see a discussion of the capital market line at https://www.wallstreetmojo.com/capital-market-line/.

Figure 4-1 Illustration of Markowitz's Efficient Frontier, Where Risk Is Measured by Standard Deviation

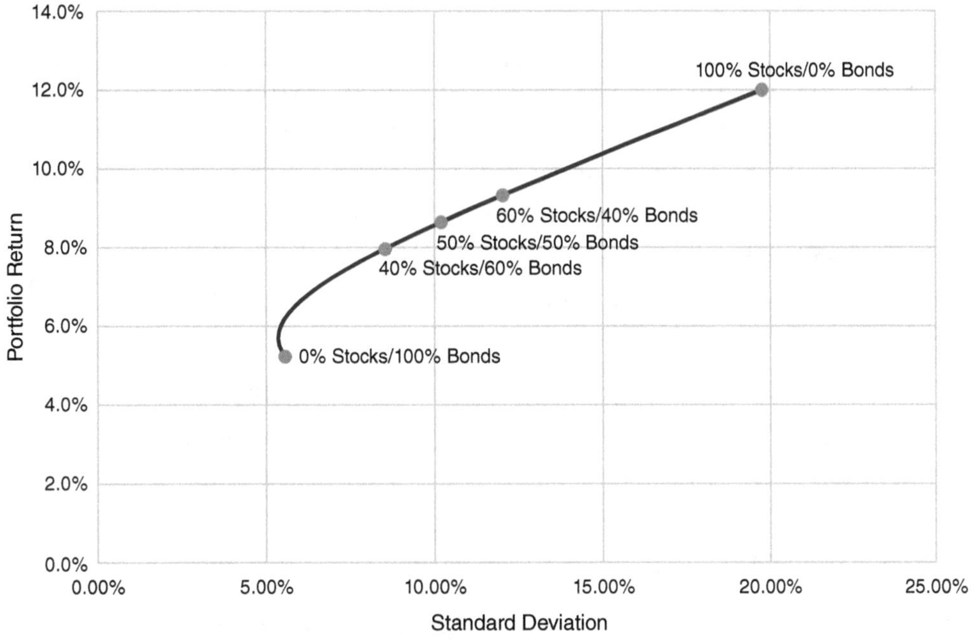

Source: Jackson, Grant. Market data is from 1926 through 2020.[6]

Note: See note to Table 2-2 for large cap stocks; Intermediate-Term Government Bond has a 2.125% coupon and five years to maturity.

How to Further Lessen Uncertainty

To minimize downside exposure further, you *could* limit your investments to short-term three-month U.S. Treasuries (T-bills). T-bills will preserve capital and generate taxable interest[7] (minimal in today's market). However, they expose you to loss of purchasing power over the long term. You would not invest in T-bills to grow your capital unless you were in

---

6. Roger G. Ibbotson, 2021 SBBI Yearbook Stocks, Bonds, Bills, and Inflation: U.S. Capital Markets Performance by Asset Class 1926–2020 (Chicago, IL: Duff & Phelps, 2021).

7. Unlike bonds, T-bills don't have coupons. They are issued by the Treasury at a discount to face value; the difference between what you pay and the amount you receive at maturity is interest, which is taxable at the federal level, but exempt from state and local income taxes. *See* Treasury Direct, https://www.treasurydirect.gov/indiv/research/indepth /tbills/res_tbill_tax.htm.

an unusual market period, such as the late 1970s and early 1980s when 12-month T-bills yielded in the double digits (as high as 17.3 percent in September of 1981).[8]

Note: In Markowitz's model, if safety is of extreme importance, you sacrifice return to decrease uncertainty. You give up growth in favor of preservation of capital. For a retiree who needs to produce cash flow for living expenses over a long horizon, additional risks need to be considered and weighed, such as loss of purchasing power due to inflation and taxes as discussed in Part II of the book.

Now, let's return to definitions for terms your adviser may use when reviewing risk trade-offs. You'll see some of these terms again in later chapters when we review reports.

MPT and PMPT Terms

The first measure to understand and use is standard deviation, which will give you a sense of volatility. A holding (or portfolio) with a higher standard deviation is more volatile than a lower standard deviation holding (or portfolio). **Standard deviation** is calculated by measuring price volatility versus the security's average price. A lower standard deviation indicates a lower return variance over a period of time, when compared to another investment with a higher standard deviation.

The **Sharpe ratio** looks at the excess returns above the risk-free rate divided by the standard deviation. When comparing investments to each other, a higher Sharpe ratio is a higher reward per unit of risk than the investment with the lower Sharpe ratio. For example, investment "A" with a Sharpe ratio of 1.2 has a better risk/reward profile than investment "B" with a Sharpe ratio of 1.0.

The **Sortino** ratio is similar to the Sharpe used by MPT, but it focuses only on the downside (price declines)—it measures the excess return per unit of downside deviation. This is PMPT's refinement of Sharpe's usage of standard deviation, which looks at both up and down movements.

---

8. *1 Year Treasury Rate—54 Year Historical Chart*, MacroTrends (2021), https://www.macrotrends.net/2492/1-year-treasury-rate-yield-chart.

When comparing two similar investments[9] to each other, *if you are risk averse*, you would be pleased with the investment with a higher Sortino ratio. For example, investment A has a Sortino ratio of 1.4; investment B has a Sortino ratio of 0.7. "A" has a better risk/reward profile than "B."

Two additional MPT measures are **Beta** and the **Treynor ratio**. Beta measures systematic risk, or the volatility of an investment compared to the market as measured by the S&P 500 Index,[10] where the market is defined by a Beta of 1. A Beta of less than 1 would indicate less risk. For example, stock with a Beta of 0.8 would be 20 percent less risky than the market. To be statistically useful, Beta needs to be measured over a longer period of time (such as three years).[11]

Treynor measures risk-adjusted returns based on Beta; the higher the Treynor ratio, the better the risk-adjusted return.

Short Illustration

To get a sense of how to apply some of these measures, let's review the 20-year period ending 2020. That time frame includes the bursting of the Internet Bubble (2000–2002), the Financial Crisis (2007–2009), the coronavirus bear (2020), and the bull markets in between.[12]

Let's focus on risk and reward using a few of these measures, namely standard deviation, Sharpe and Sortino ratios, and maximum drawdown.

---

9. An example of investments would be two comparable stocks in the same sector and industry with similar market caps or two high-yield bond mutual funds or two U.S. small capitalization mutual funds.

10. Some calculate Beta against other benchmarks; be sure to check. See Morningtar and YCharts.

11. "While beta has limited predictive reliability for any one security over short time periods, it has been found to be highly useful as a forecasting tool over longer periods for well diversified equity portfolios, like most mutual funds. . . . The only caveat is that "investments with low correlation to the index (low r-squared, e.g., less than 0.30–0.50), have betas that are not very meaningful and should not be relied upon." *STEELE Mutual Fund Expert User Guide*. Reports, graphs, analysis, and data generated with STEELE Mutual Fund Expert Software, www.MutualFundExpert.com. Copyright © Steele Systems, Inc. 2021. All rights reserved.

12. See Chapter 3 for 21-year results. See Note to Table 2-2 for bull and bear markets.

Four Portfolios

Let's review four different types of portfolios, from least risk to most risk. Based on risk-avoidance alone, an investor might choose to preserve savings with treasury or money market investments (Fund A). Someone who is willing to take on more risk might choose a balanced, stock and bond portfolio (Fund B, STEELE's Balanced Average). A more risk-tolerant investor might choose to replicate the S&P 500 Index (Fund C). And a risk-on investor might want to invest in small capitalization stocks (Fund D).

First, standard deviation. As you can see from Table 4-1, the funds are arrayed as you would expect based on their objectives, from lower to higher risk: Fund A with the lowest standard deviation and Fund D with the highest. Note that the S&P 500 was significantly more volatile than A and B and less volatile than D for the 20-year period.

Table 4-1 Standard Deviation[13] (12/31/2000–12/31/2020)

Objective	T-bills	Balanced	S&P 500	Small Cap
Fund	A	B	C	D
Standard Deviation 20-year	1.7	9.5	14.8	19.3

Judging the funds *solely* on this volatility measure, Fund A would have been the best choice of the four for the most risk-averse investor, with the lowest standard deviation.

Sharpe and Sortino Ratios

Next, we'll see how risk-adjusted ratios compare, keeping in mind that the higher the Sharpe (and Sortino) ratios, the better the risk-adjusted return. These ratios are outcomes (returns on a risk-adjusted basis using standard deviation and downside deviation as measures). Compare the Sharpe ratios in Table 4-2: Fund A at 0.8, B at 0.5, C at 0.6, and D at 0.5. Compare the Sortino ratios: Fund A at 1.4, B at 0.7, C at 0.8, and D at 0.8.

---

13. Data sourced from STEELE Mutual Fund Expert Software, www.MutualFund Expert.com. Copyright © Steele Systems, Inc. 2021. All rights reserved. Reproduced with permission. (20 year periods vs. 21 in Chapter 3). Fund B is STEELE's Balanced Average.

Table 4-2 Sharpe and Sortino Ratios[14] (12/31/2000–12/31/2020)

Objective	T-bills	Balanced	S&P 500	Small Cap
Fund	A	B	C	D
Sharpe 20-year	0.8	0.5	0.6	0.5
Sortino 20-year	1.4	0.7	0.8	0.8

Again, judging the funds *solely* on these two measures, looking back over the 20-year history, Fund A would have produced the best outcome of the four for the very conservative risk-averse investor, with the highest Sharpe and Sortino ratios.

Another risk measure looks back over the time frame to see how much each portfolio or holding fell in price from a previous peak.

Maximum Drawdowns

The best way to measure a historical percentage decline is a data point called "maximum drawdown" (see Table 4-3). Drawdowns represent the percentage the investor would have lost, if the investment had been purchased at its peak value and sold at the rock-bottom of a peak to trough decline.

Table 4-3 Maximum Drawdowns (%)[15] (12/31/2000–12/31/2020)

Objective	T-bills	Balanced	S&P 500	Small Cap
Fund	A	B	C	D
Maximum Drawdown (%) 20-years	–1.5	–35.6	–51.0	–53.8

Note that the smallest drawdown was experienced by the least volatile investment (Fund A), followed by the next least volatile (Fund B), and so on. As you might expect, the two more volatile investments (Funds C and D) also had the largest drawdowns.

You'll see how lower risk translates into lower returns next.

---

14. *Id*. Note: Fund B is STEELE's Balanced Average.
15. *Id*. Note: Fund B is STEELE's Balanced Average.

Twenty-Year Returns

Average annual returns (Table 4-4) followed long-horizon risk versus reward trade-off expectations: Fund A at 3.1 percent, B at 6.1 percent, C at 7.3 percent, and D at 9.1 percent average annual returns.[16]

Table 4-4 Average Annual Returns without Withdrawals (12/31/2000–12/31/2020)

Objective	T-bills	Balanced	S&P 500	Small Cap
Fund	A	B	C	D
Average Annual Returns (%) 20 years	3.1	6.1	7.3	9.1

Context for Retirees: Risk versus Return

With the benefit of hindsight, Fund D would have been the best choice for any investor seeking the highest returns. However, Fund D owners' experience over those 20 years would have been, shall I say, "most exciting," with a decline of more than 50 percent during the worst downward period.

The key question for a retiree to consider is this: If you had owned Fund D (or C), would you have been able to stomach those drawdowns? That's a question that can be answered "yes" in the calm of historical analysis. But how would you have answered that question in the heat of a market event like the 2020 coronavirus decline? Recall that the S&P 500 declined 34 percent in a little over a month (February 19, 2020 to March 23, 2020).

In real life, the investment would need to support withdrawals to fuel living expenses. When that happens, interim volatility negatively impacts value. Drawdowns can be significant for more volatile holdings such as Fund C and Fund D—and impactful if they occur at the beginning of retirement.

Any long-term investor will benefit from studying an investment to determine risk first, potential reward second, before a portfolio is structured.

---

16. *Id.* Note: Fund B is STEELE's Balanced Average.

Adding Risk through Leverage

Let's turn to other risks that need to be understood when managing a portfolio. Since a company can go out of business, an investment in a stock or bond can go to zero. With some investments, you can lose more than you invest. For example, if you buy a stock on margin, write options, sell a stock short, or buy or sell futures contracts, you are borrowing money from the brokerage firm to execute the transaction.

When working with an investment adviser, it's important to get clarification about leverage. I do *not* recommend using leverage, with the exception, under *very limited circumstances*, of certain leveraged investment vehicles[17] where your loss is limited to the amount invested, not more.

Liquidity Restrictions

Another risk to assess is not being able to get to your money. For example, investment products with surrender charges might discourage you from liquidating until after the end of the surrender period.[18] Private equity funds may impose restrictions on withdrawals for a number of years (ten years, for example).[19] Liquidity is of particular concern if you are depending on your investments as a source of retirement cash flow. Depending on the security, a fund prospectus,[20] an offering circular, a fact

---

17. Examples are leveraged closed-end funds and leveraged ETFs.

18. For example, a variable annuity or mutual fund with a contingent deferred sales charge for redemptions made within a certain period of time from the date of purchase might cause investors to wait until the surrender charge goes to zero. For a description of deferred sales charges and redemption fees, read the SEC's *Investor Bulletin: Mutual Fund Fees and Expenses*, https://www.investor.gov/introduction-investing /general-resources/news-alerts/alerts-bulletins/investor-bulletins-20.

19. https://www.investor.gov/introduction-investing/investing-basics/investment -products/private-investment-funds/private-equity.

20. You can search for prospectuses on the SEC's EDGAR website at https://www .investor.gov/introduction-investing/getting-started/researching-investments/using -edgar-research-investments.

- The SEC's Investor.gov website provides a three-part guide on how to read a prospectus.
- Read Part 1 of 3 at https://www.investor.gov/introduction-investing/general-res ources/news-alerts/alerts-bulletins/investor-bulletins/how-read-2.
- Part 2 of 3 at https://www.investor.gov/introduction-investing/general-resources /news-alerts/alerts-bulletins/investor-bulletins/how-read-0.
- Part 3 of 3 at https://www.investor.gov/introduction-investing/general-resources /news-alerts/alerts-bulletins/investor-bulletins/how-read-1.

sheet, or a Morningstar[21] report can provide information on these potential liquidity restrictions.

Key Takeaways

How does risk fit into your goals? From my perspective, *all* retirement
portfolios need to address risk tolerance (how much volatility you can live
with over long and short periods of time) as well as risk capacity (how
much you can afford to lose in dollars at any point in time, should you
decide to sell). My view is that every portfolio should provide a mecha-
nism for preserving capital, even in situations when risk appetite is high.

But there is more: A retiree faces much greater risks than the risk of
a poor investment or a market drop. The big risk is failing to maintain
a desired lifestyle, in the worst case, outliving one's resources. That risk
needs to be addressed by the investment adviser before a portfolio can be
constructed.

This is another distinguishing factor between advisers. It's where
expertise and planning come together. It starts with a question: If you
have a retirement income gap (see Chapter 1) that needs to be filled from
the portfolio, how will that cash flow be generated now, and in the future,
while building capital for a legacy? That's the investment challenge that
needs to be defined and answered, which brings us to a focus on you, the
subject of Part II of the book.

Read the SEC's *Information Available to Investment Company Shareholders*, at
https://www.investor.gov/introduction-investing/investing-basics/glossary/information
-available-investment-company.

21. Morningstar products provide proprietary data, independent research, investment strategies, and analytics.

PART II
Personal Portfolio Management Principles

In Part I of this book, we reviewed market history and foundational concepts, including a special focus on market and investment risk. Now, we need to turn to another type of risk, the risk of an individual not being able to maintain a desired lifestyle, in the worst case, outliving his or her resources. To prepare to address this risk, we need to study *you*—to bring you into the "personal" part of the portfolio management equation that we discussed in Chapter 1.

In doing so, let me remind you that retirement investing is nothing like the type of investing that people engage in during their working careers. Then, the goal was simple: save for a future need; invest for capital appreciation. In retirement, much more is involved.

Depending on your personal situation, you may need to create your own pension-like cash flow to support yourself through retirement, unless your employer pension plan satisfies that need. You may have legacy and charitable interests. You may be in your sixties with a 30-year investment horizon, or you may be older and looking to grow your assets for the next generation. Single, married, children, grandchildren, blended families, incapacities, health issues, real property, collectibles, farm land, business interests—all of the idiosyncratic factors make us all different in terms of financial needs and desires.

Because of the diversity of individual situations, it is almost impossible to run a retirement portfolio based on rules of thumb, such as set asset allocations based on age, set withdrawal rates, or even when to buy or sell holdings.

What's the answer? The subject of Part II of the book: a customized portfolio that is tailored to fit your needs—which are, after all, unique to you.

Note: In this part of the book, you'll see references to "investment advisers." I'm using that term to include investment advisers that are stand-alone firms as well as dual registrants that provide both advisory and brokerage services. These topics will be discussed in Part III. *Importantly, as you read ahead, if you plan to manage your own portfolio, think of* yourself *as the investment adviser.*

Chapter 5
Turning Inward: Understanding Cash Flow Prepares You for the Future

In Part I of the book, we talked about the risk an investor takes on in the financial marketplace. When a retiree thinks of risk, the landscape of financial decisions is much larger than the risk of losing money in the market. We're talking about preserving a lifestyle throughout retirement. The key to mitigating this very personal and very real risk is understanding your personal cash flow, the topic of this chapter.

Cash Flow Drives

Only after cash flow is understood, can you consider how to turn savings into a strategically organized portfolio that fuels withdrawals—a topic that could be missed by investors who have never retired before (see Source of Funding Portfolio Withdrawals). An ancillary issue is how to judge whether your portfolio can withstand the withdrawals you would like to make (see The 4 Percent Rule?; Taxes; Monte Carlo Simulations & Sensitivity Analyses).

Before we begin, let me lay some groundwork. First, we're talking *cash flow*: money coming into the household (inflow) and money leaving the household (outflow). And, we're talking about the present (current expenses, income, and assets) and the future (inflation, taxes, time horizon, changing needs, returns on investment, and the like).

There are many financial planning tools available for the retail and the institutional markets that take these variables and others into account when looking into the future—they give you an outcome to consider.

This chapter does something different. Instead of an outcome, expect this chapter to leave you with an idea of the preparatory work that precedes the structuring of a retirement portfolio. Again, the driver is household cash flow.

Expectations

When it comes to expenses in retirement, the U.S. Department of Labor[1] (DOL) provides some guidance on expectations. The DOL estimates that you'll need at least 70 percent of your annual preretirement income to cover your annual retirement expenses. Some experts cited by the DOL say more—80 to 90 percent.[2] This rule of thumb does not apply in all situations, of course. For example, if you plan on traveling more after you retire, you will need to increase your estimate. Also, the estimate is based on today's dollars. You will need to adjust it for year-to-year increases in the cost of living due to inflation, as we will discuss in the Inflation Expectations section later in this chapter.

Household Cash Outflow: Living Expenses

Calculating current living expenses is straightforward. By living expenses, I mean ordinary everyday costs of living, including housing, real estate taxes, medical care, transportation, food, entertainment, and the like. There are a number of tools available online[3] that can help start the exercise. If you would like to know where you stand compared to the U.S. population, the Bureau of Labor Statistics[4] provides household data.

For a starting point, one would exclude one-time (nonrecurring) expenses and income taxes, since income taxes will depend in part on portfolio construction. Nonrecurring items include home improvement projects, weddings, and gifts to grandchildren. These items are added back into the equation once you know how much you spend annually.

---

1. *Taking the Mystery Out of Retirement Planning*, U.S. DEP'T OF LABOR (Nov. 2018), https://www.dol.gov/sites/dolgov/files/ebsa/about-ebsa/our-activities/resource-center/publications/taking-the-mystery-out-of-retirement-planning.pdf.

2. *Id.* at 18.

3. Quicken's Budget Calculator is an example. Access the site at quicken.com/budget-calculator.

4. The U.S. Bureau of Labor Statistics publishes household expenditure data ("Consumer Expenditure Surveys"), which you can find at bls.gov/cex/.

Essential versus Discretionary Expenses

Watch for this nuance to help with future decisions: When calculating how much you are spending on various expense categories, be conscious of whether the expenses are for needs (essential expenses) or wants (discretionary expenses). Discretionary expenses are those you can live without if need be, such as gifts, vacations, and entertainment. That's an important distinction for a retiree—while discretionary expenses can be delayed, normally, essential expenses cannot.

Major life changes and disruptions can make projecting expenses a challenge—especially changes of a traumatic nature, like the incapacity or the loss of a spouse. If you find yourself feeling uncertain about your projected expenses, especially in the wake of changes, consider consulting your accountant for assistance.

The number you arrive at for your living expenses will normally not equal the dollar amount to withdraw from savings to satisfy your lifestyle needs in retirement. They are two different figures, as you will see when we discuss the Retirement Income Gap later in this chapter.

Note: How much you actually need to withdraw from the portfolio in a year and in the future will help the investment adviser determine the optimal structure of the portfolio.[5] Taxes and non-routine expenses will need to be figured and added into the equation later, as portfolio construction will affect income taxes.

The next part of the exercise to determine future cash flow needs is calculating the effect of inflation.

Inflation Expectations

To get a sense of what one might experience in the future when it comes to inflation, history is a guide but not a perfect measure, as economies change due to technological and other advances. Since 1913, annual

---

5. I'm using the term investment adviser in this chapter to pick up firms registered solely as investment advisers (stand-alone advisers) as well as dual registrants, but leaving out stand-alone broker-dealers. We will discuss these terms in Part III of the book.

inflation as measured by the Consumer Price Index (CPI) has included deflationary periods and double-digit inflationary periods.

Comparing single years, the lowest measure of the Consumer Price Index (CPI) was a –10.5 percent in 1921. The highest inflationary measure was 18.0 percent in 1918. We've seen double-digit inflation as recently as 1981 (10.3 percent), 1980 (13.5 percent), 1979 (11.3 percent), and 1974 (11.0 percent).[6]

During a shorter historical time frame, after World War II (1945–2020), one-year swings were more restrained, but still included deflationary periods and double-digit inflation. The greatest one-year deflationary reading during this period was –1.2 percent in 1949.[7] The highest one-year inflationary reading was 14.4 percent in 1947. For the year 2020, the inflation rate was 1.20 percent.[8] In 2021, the inflation rate increased to 7 percent, as many areas of the economy experienced limited supply versus increased demand as a result of COVID-19 shutdowns.[9]

In order to match a possible horizon for a 65-year-old person, 30-year historical periods might be more telling. During the lowest 30-year period, inflation averaged 0.7 percent per year (12/31/1919 to 12/31/1949). The median was 3.3 percent per year (12/31/1947 to 12/31/1977). The highest was 5.4 percent per year (12/31/1965 to 12/31/1995).[10]

Shortening the 30-year period to post-World War II (12/31/1944 to 12/31/2020) gives us a different inflation perspective. The lowest 30-year period was 2.3 percent per year (12/31/1990 to 12/31/2020).[11] The median was 4.3 percent per year (12/31/1952 to 12/31/1982).[12] The highest remains at 5.4 percent per year (12/31/1965 to 12/31/1995).[13]

---

6. *Historical Inflation Rates: 1914–2021*, US Inflation Calculator (May 12, 2021), https://www.usinflationcalculator.com/inflation/historical-inflation-rates/. Data is based on CPI returns (rate of inflation) using the Consumer Price Index published by the Bureau of Labor Statistics, https://www.bls.gov/cpi/home.htm.

7. *Id.*

8. *Id.*

9. *Id.*

10. Capital Group Hypothetical calculates 30-year rolling CPI returns (rate of inflation) using the Consumer Price Index published by the U.S. Bureau of Labor Statistics, https://www.bls.gov/cpi/home.htm.

11. *Id.*

12. *Id.*

13. *Id.*

What does this mean in practical terms? When you model expenses over long periods, such as retirement that might last 30 years or longer, you do need to account for inflation.

As an example, using 3 percent inflation, your buying power would be cut in half in 24 years. If your expenses were $100,000 at age 65, at age 89 you would need $200,000 to pay for the same goods you paid $100,000 for at age 65.

If inflation were 6 percent per year over a 30-year period, your age 65 buying power would be cut in half by age 77, when you would need $200,000 to pay for $100,000 of age 65 expenses, and you would need $400,000 when you are 89.

The next part of the puzzle is how to factor in the effect of taxes.

Note: Retirees will need to address taxes triggered by required minimum distributions from tax-deferred retirement accounts, such as IRAs. The owner of the IRA is required to start RMDs at age 72 (changed from 70½ by the SECURE Act (the Setting Every Community Up for Retirement Enhancement Act of 2019)). The SECURE Act also severely limited inheritors' ability to stretch an inherited IRA, an important planning point for retirees, and the subject of a digital download (see introduction).

Taxes

Consider three types of tax assumptions. First, *the individual's effective tax rate*[14] is assumed based on the current tax structure and most recent tax return (with known adjustments), with the understanding that tax rates and structure will likely change in the future. Second, portfolio strategy will need to consider *how individual investments are taxed*, including an analysis of unrealized gains imbedded in current holdings and different rates that apply to tax-advantaged investments, such as municipal

---

14. The effective tax rate is the percentage of income paid in taxes, which gives models a more exact read on tax outflow than tax brackets. Brackets can be helpful when planning to add to income, as when considering a Roth conversion.

bonds and qualified dividends.[15] Third, anyone with tax-deferred retirement accounts will need to factor in *taxes that are triggered by mandatory withdrawals* (required minimum distributions, or RMDs[16]). There are a number of ways to factor taxes into the cash flow equation; make sure you understand your adviser's method.

Nonroutine Outflow

Other types of withdrawals are the nonroutine amounts that also need to be funded from time to time. Some investment advisers might want to set up a separate account held in cash equivalents for such purposes. (Be sure to ask how your adviser handles additional withdrawals above your monthly needs.)

Now let's turn to the inflow part of the cash flow equation. First, we'll discuss non-portfolio income, then savings.

Note: Don't lump together non-portfolio income with returns on investments or RMDs at this point; it's too early in the process.

Inflow from Non-Portfolio Income

On the income side of the cash flow equation is non-portfolio income from "guaranteed" sources, such as pensions and Social Security retirement benefits. While Social Security[17] decisions are outside the scope of this book, here are two things to remember. First, Social Security benefits are indexed to inflation, while most pensions are not. Second, if you are married, address the potential loss or reduction of Social Security income (and pension) when one spouse predeceases the other. Adding together

---

15. Publication 550: Investment Income and Expenses (Cat. No. 15093R), U.S. Dep't of the Treasury, Internal Revenue Service (2020), https://www.irs.gov/pub/irs-prior /p550--2020.pdf.

16. The subject of RMDs is covered in IRS Publication 590-B. While RMD details are outside the scope of this book, I've provided key IRA resources in the Suggested Reading section in the back of this book and a digital download on the subject (see introduction).

17. Social Security records can be downloaded from ssa.gov/myaccount/. For a discussion of Social Security, see Avram Sacks, *Strategizing Your Social Security Claim*, *in* Second Acts for Solo and Small Firm Lawyers 193–230 (Jennifer J. Rose ed., ABA Publishing 2019).

the pensions and Social Security benefits that you will receive in the first year of retirement will give you a sense of "guaranteed" sources of income that are produced outside of savings.

Note: "Savings" refers to assets before they are invested into a goal-driven retirement portfolio.

The Retirement Income Gap

After comparing outflows to inflows from non-portfolio income, you'll have a sense of how to deploy savings. First, you'll need to solve for the dollar amount you'll need to tap, assuming the outflow is greater than the inflow. For example, if your inflow (non-portfolio income) is $100,000 and you are spending $300,000 on living expenses, you need to pull $200,000 from your savings. While your expenses come to $300,000, your retirement income gap is $200,000. That's the number to solve for when constructing a retirement portfolio in year one of retirement.

Arriving at the retirement income gap leads us to the most important part of this exercise: Determining whether your savings can be turned into a goal-driven portfolio that satisfies your lifetime lifestyle needs and legacy wishes.

The Role of Savings: After-Tax Returns

At this point, the dollar amount of your savings (by type of account, whether taxable or tax-deferred) needs to be incorporated into the picture. Projections into the future will need to capture forced withdrawals from tax-deferred accounts after age 72 (RMDs)[18] and to compute cash flows after the effect of taxes on those withdrawals and on holdings in taxable accounts.

Your investment adviser will likely use financial planning software to run projections. There are a number of financial planning software services available to the retail market that can be helpful if you are a do-it-yourselfer.

---

18. RMDs are required minimum distributions for tax-deferred accounts as discussed in IRS Publication 590-B.

Note: Software vendors offer different ways to project after-tax returns (and other variables) into the future. Be sure to check with your adviser on the method used in your projections. Be especially cautious about the effect of compounding over longer periods of time.

Return assumptions will flow from the methodology the adviser intends to use when constructing a retirement portfolio. That is, potential returns flow from how the portfolio is structured. Let's turn to some possibilities.

Source of Funding Portfolio Withdrawals

No matter the situation, if a client needs to withdraw funds from his or her portfolio to pay for living expenses, the investment adviser must determine an appropriate methodology to support the withdrawals for a lifetime sufficient to adjust for changes in living expenses, and offsetting inflation and taxes.

The methodology the adviser intends to use needs to be articulated. If your adviser doesn't mention it, be sure to ask. You can expect one or more variations of the following:

1. Income only. Cash flow is produced from the income (dividends and interest) generated by the portfolio.
2. Capital appreciation only. Cash flow is produced by liquidating positions. (Investors who experienced bull market returns before retirement need to be especially cautious about their expectations.)
3. Total return (combination of income and capital appreciation). Cash flow is produced in part by liquidating principal and in part by the creation of income.
4. "Guaranteed" income through the purchase of an immediate annuity, creating a pension-like cash flow stream. This approach is typically offered by a financial planner who is licensed to sell insurance (immediate annuities are insurance contracts issued by insurance companies; the sale of immediate annuities is regulated by the individual states; immediate annuities are not securities). The immediate annuity is purchased with a lump-sum payment (premium) to

produce payouts. Options are available, such as payments for a "period certain" if the annuitant dies within for example, ten years after the purchase; joint and survivor payments; payments with inflation adjustments to offset inflation over time.

5. Combination of annuity and total return. One method is to create a payout from an immediate annuity to cover essential expenses, leaving the remainder of the assets to be run on a total return basis.

6. Combinations of any of the above, with cash segregation. Another method is to set aside a certain amount of cash to use in anticipation of the next market decline. Any time there is cash segregation, consider the lost opportunity cost of not having those funds invested.

To reiterate, no matter who you work with, it is essential to understand the adviser's (or your own) methodology for producing your portfolio withdrawals. (This is one of the distinguishing characteristics between advisers.) Will those amounts be supported by income produced by the portfolio, the liquidation of positions, a cash reserve, an annuity purchased from an insurance company, or another source? Why do you want to know? You need to judge whether you agree with the methodology—to determine whether it is suitable for your needs and sustainable.

Note: Be aware that when you need to sell holdings to pay for expenses, you open yourself up to additional decision points, for example, when and what to sell. Caution is in order: If you hit down-market periods, especially if they occur in the early years of your retirement, you are most at risk of prematurely depleting savings by selling declining positions to fund expenses.

If the method used involves selling holdings, you will need to familiarize yourself with safe withdrawal rates if they are being relied on by the adviser (or you). Let's discuss that now.

The 4 Percent Rule?

Retirement income literature suggests that a safe withdrawal rate of 4.0 or 4.5 percent of your savings might be an appropriate guide. The 4.0

percent figure originated with William Bengen who wrote a 1994 article entitled "Determining Withdrawal Rates Using Historical Data."[19]

Bengen used historical stock and bond market returns published by Ibbotson in the *Stocks, Bonds, Bills and Inflation 1992 Yearbook*. He tested a 50 percent stock and 50 percent intermediate-term treasury-bond portfolio, incorporating inflation, over 30-year rolling periods (starting 1926 through 1976). His goal was to learn what percentage allocation would survive all 30-year holding periods in the time frame he studied.

Note: Bengen's analysis did *not* include the effect of taxes or trading costs.

Bengen concluded that:

[A]ssuming a minimum requirement of 30 years of portfolio longevity, a first-year withdrawal of 4 percent, followed by inflation-adjusted withdrawals in subsequent years should be safe. In no past case has it caused a portfolio to be exhausted before 33 years, and in most cases, it will lead to portfolio lives of 50 years or longer.[20]

In the years following his 1994 publication, Bengen adjusted the withdrawal rate to 4.5 percent of the initial value, added other holdings, and named the rule "SAFEMAX."

Subsequently, a number of people updated Bengen's study over time, including Bengen himself, in a paper published on October 1, 2020.[21] There, he addressed a different question. He pointed out that SAFEMAX focused on the worst-case scenario, which happened to be

---

19. William Bengen, *Determining Withdrawal Rates Using Historical Data*, 71(1) J. Fin. Plan. 171–80 (1994), https://www.financialplanningassociation.org/sites/default /files/2021-04/MAR04%20Determining%20Withdrawal%20Rates%20Using%20His torical%20Data.pdf.

20. *Id.*

21. William P. Bengen, *Choosing the Highest Safe Withdrawal Rate at Retirement*, Fin. Adviser Mag., Oct. 1, 2020, https://www.fa-mag.com/news/choosing-the-highest -safe-withdrawal-rate-at-retirement-58132.html.

the 30 years beginning October 1, 1968 (due to high inflation and poor stock market returns).

Bengen looked at how more favorable market conditions could lead to higher withdrawals above 4.5 percent. In the new analysis, allocations were adjusted as follows: the percentage of large capitalization stocks was reduced from 50 to 30 percent, with 20 percent U.S. small cap stocks making up the difference.

Looking at the question from this different perspective, he noted that:

> [T]here were many occasions in the past when withdrawal rates higher than even 5.5 percent could have been successfully employed. In fact, the average SAFEMAX for all retirement for the years 1926 to 1990 was 7.0 percent, much higher than the 'worst case' scenario of 4.5 percent.[22]

Bengen incorporated work done by Michael Kitces in the 2008 Kitces Report that utilized the Shiller CAPE (the *C*yclically *A*djusted *P*rice-*E*arnings ratio for the S&P 500 Index). Bengen concluded that incorporating the CAPE would allow investors to assess when they could increase their withdrawal rates beyond 4.5 percent.

While history is a useful guide, Bengen ended with this "cheerful disclaimer" worth noting:

> I should also issue the usual cheerful disclaimer that this research is based on the analysis of historical data, and its application to future situations involves risk, as the future may differ significantly from the past. The term "safe" is meaningful only in its historical context, and does not imply a guarantee of future applicability.[23]

Indeed, there are no guarantees. However, there are guideposts and there are ways to monitor performance to see if history is replaying the past or whether another strategy needs to be put in place. In any event, the market period that you "own" will be determinative of your experience. You won't know *in advance* what that market period will look like.

---

22. *Id.*
23. Bengen, *supra* note 21.

Note: For a good discussion of different "safe withdrawal rate" methods, read Morningstar's, "The State of Retirement Income," released November 11, 2021.[24] Morningstar recognizes that: "Helping pre-retirees and retirees to determine the "right" withdrawal rate for retirement is one of the trickiest jobs in financial planning."[25]

Instead of searching for the ideal safe withdrawal rate, which is an exercise in predicting the future, some investment advisers reverse the inquiry by starting with you instead of starting with a number. That method first identifies your cash flow demands, then considers how a portfolio can be structured to meet those demands now and into the future, after taxes and inflation (see Chapter 7).

Given the variety in methodology, expect the adviser you retain to manage your portfolio to clearly define the philosophy of the firm in how to meet withdrawal needs. (You'll need to confirm that your adviser provides that service.)

Caution: Don't Forget Taxes

Before relying on either the 4 or 4.5 percent figure (or any other), let me remind you that *neither* figure in Bengen's study is *after* taxes. As a result, these guideposts are limited to tax-free accounts, such as Roth IRAs. (Tax-deferred IRAs *do* need to capture taxes on withdrawals, most importantly, mandated withdrawals after age 72[26] (required minimum distributions or RMDs).) As Bengen stated, "the analysis for a taxable account would be considerably more complex."[27] (Now, software such as *Morningstar® Advisor Workstation*[SM] can incorporate income tax assumptions into the equation.)

---

24. https://www.morningstar.com/articles/1066569/whats-a-safe-retirement-spending-rate-for-the-decades-ahead.

25. Christine Benz, Jeffrey Ptak & John Rekenthaler, *The State of Retirement Income: Safe Withdrawal Rates*, Morningstar (Nov. 2021).

26. The Setting Every Community Up for Retirement Enhancement Act of 2019 (SECURE Act), changed the age at which IRA owners are required to start RMDs from age 70½ to age 72.

27. William Bengen, *Determining Withdrawal Rates Using Historical Data*, 71(1) J. Fin. Plan. 171–80, Appendix (1994).

Note: Here are some questions for you: In order to rely on the 4 or 4.5 percent (or other) safe withdrawal rule, how would you need to structure your portfolio? How would you factor in taxes? How would you plan your withdrawals? Assume you need a monthly "paycheck" from the portfolio to pay your bills. What would you sell? When would you decide to make the sale? What would you sell if your holdings were all declining at the same time? How would you protect your savings against erosion?

Monte Carlo Simulations

Investment advisers might use Monte Carlo simulations to assess the probabilities of success or ruin of an existing portfolio or a recommended portfolio. Monte Carlo simulations[28] use thousands of randomized simulations to produce the probability of success (such as having a positive value at age 100). The number of successes divided by the number of simulations gives you the probability of success. They are named for Monte Carlo, Monaco, known for its gambling casinos.

Three points need to be made: First, be sure to check assumptions. For example, not all Monte Carlos factor in withdrawals—you would want to know that. Some that do, figure withdrawals at year end as a single withdrawal, but grow the portfolio throughout the year, which would result in a more favorable result than a model that reduces the portfolio as withdrawals are made monthly. Second, consider how the result is reported. That is, does it satisfy you to know that you have, say, an 85 percent chance of success of not running out of money? Third, there is another method, a cash flow sensitivity analysis, which may be helpful either together with a Monte Carlo or on its own.

Cash Flow Sensitivity Analysis

The cash flow inputs that we discussed give you control of the sensitivity analysis. One can factor an array of different assumptions for cash

---

28. If you want to check out a Monte Carlo simulations program on your own, there are some available for the retail market. For example, Maxifiplanner.com offers a version that includes Monte Carlo simulations. Also see Palisade's @ RISK or Frontline Systems' Risk Solver (add-ons to Microsoft Excel).

outflows, non-portfolio income, taxes, after-tax RMDs, inflation, and different returns, projected out over time. The results provide a range of outcomes to compare to each other.

I firmly believe that one should not attempt structuring a retirement portfolio without a cash flow sensitivity analysis, and further, that the analysis should be repeated periodically to remain relevant as life evolves.

Avoid Portfolio Construction Shortcuts

Some might recommend a portfolio based on shortcuts such as, a formulaic allocation (60 percent stocks; 40 percent bonds) to be rebalanced periodically; 100 minus your age for your percentage stock allocation (if you are 60 years old, 100 minus 60 would give you a 40 percent stock allocation, with the rest in bonds); keeping savings in a bank account; buying a retirement income product; among others. It would be hard to convince me that shortcuts are worthwhile except *perhaps* where savings and expenses are modest and time horizon short.

Creating a retirement portfolio is simply not a one-size-fits-all endeavor. It will be up to you to decide whether your situation calls for more or less preparatory work. My preference? I would do the work.

Key Takeaways

Cash flow drives the retirement planning equation, solving for this question: How much cash needs to be withdrawn from savings to preserve lifestyle during retirement. That's the clarifying question that precedes all others. The answer gives you a foundation upon which to build a retirement portfolio.

Once that is determined, the adviser has a problem to solve: What is the optimal method to use to fund withdrawals while meeting other portfolio goals. One adviser's approach will differ from another's, and that is one of the differentiating factors between advisers . . . food for thought when in the market for a retirement adviser.

Consequently, when an investment adviser presents a strategy (or you yourself create one), you need to understand the philosophy and process that will direct the construction and management of the portfolio.

Among the things to be considered:

- What are your current living expenses and how might they change over time?
- What is the plan on how to fill the retirement income gap (if any) between your non-portfolio income (Social Security and pensions) and your needs?
- What is the methodology that underpins the production of withdrawals from your portfolio? Are the withdrawals coming from income generated by the portfolio or by liquidating principal or an outside source of income such as an annuity?
- Before relying on a safe withdrawal rate, consider doing a sensitivity analysis at different after-tax rates of return.
- What is the plan on how to address income and capital gains taxes and inflation?
- What is the game plan for handling required minimum distributions from tax-deferred accounts?
- Is the proposed plan customized to your situation or a product solution that is offered to anyone who is retiring? Do you need a tailored portfolio?

In the next chapter, we'll discuss how to formulate investment objectives. Then, in Chapter 7, we'll go to the next step of pulling together information you need to address how you will manage your retirement portfolio based on whether you have a retirement income gap.

Chapter 6
Creating Investment Objectives

Now, let us turn to how an investment advisory firm will transform what it knows about you into an Investment Policy Statement (IPS) that will guide the portfolio for the present and potentially for years to come.

The creation of an IPS invites a dialogue between you and your investment adviser about your objectives and the firm's strategies for achieving them. As such, it is a highly valuable exercise. And, an IPS is another point of differentiation between firms and their representatives—something to talk about when choosing an adviser.

Investment Policy Statement

The investment advisory firm you engage will likely craft an IPS that demonstrates the firm's plan on how it will meet your needs.[1] I say "likely," since there is no regulatory requirement to provide an IPS and there is no standard IPS used in the industry. Some investment advisers provide an IPS to all clients, while some provide a written IPS only to clients with more complex situations, opting for verbal discussion for simpler situations.

Should you receive an IPS, it will be important for you to read, understand, and agree (or disagree) with this document after providing feedback during its conceptualization. The example that follows will help prepare you to do that.

---

1. Kurt Schacht, James Allen & Robert Dannhauser, Elements of an Investment Policy Statement for Individual Investors 1 (CFA Inst. 2010), https://www.cfainstitute.org/-/media/documents/article/position-paper/investment-policy-statement-individual-investors.ashx.

An Example

While my firm's IPS takes a different path, let me share a good example of a basic IPS for retirees provided courtesy of Morningstar, Inc.[2] The Morningstar sample IPS[3] covers these five sections: a purpose statement, a client summary, a proposed portfolio, a monitoring statement, and the client's acceptance of the IPS. In the rest of this chapter, I'll share Morningstar's descriptions of each section.

Purpose Statement

The purpose of an investment policy statement is to:

- Establish objectives for structuring an investment proposal suitable to [your] long-term needs and risk tolerance.
- Formulate policies for selecting appropriate and suitable investments within the framework of that structure.
- Establish prudent procedures for monitoring and evaluating the performance of investments within the proposal and for addressing changes in policy.[4]

Next, the IPS recaps the prior work done in preparation of the IPS.

This document identifies information that was gathered from [you] for purposes of formulating an investment proposal. The information sought from [you] addresses [your] intentions and goals, and financial constraints that may impact the proposal. In

---

2. Morningstar products provide proprietary data, independent research, investment strategies, and analytics.

3. The IPS quoted here is reproduced with permission from Morningstar. © 2021 Morningstar, Inc. All Rights Reserved. The information contained herein: (1) is proprietary to Morningstar and/or its content providers; (2) may not be copied or distributed; (3) does not constitute investment advice offered by Morningstar; and (4) is not warranted to be accurate, complete, or timely. Neither Morningstar nor its content providers are responsible for any damages or losses arising from any use of this information. Past performance is no guarantee of future results. Use of information from Morningstar does not necessarily constitute agreement by Morningstar, Inc. of any investment philosophy or strategy presented in this publication.

4. Data sourced from © 2021 Morningstar, Inc. All Rights Reserved. Reproduced with permission. *Creating Batch Reports and the Investment Policy Statements*, at 2, advisor.morningstar.com/Principia/pdf/BatchReports_IPS%20Statement.pdf.

addition, it identifies a target asset allocation of investment types and weightings that the investment proposal will endeavor to apply to meet [your] long-term objectives. Finally, it proposes an agenda for reconsidering the overall structure for the plan, as well as security implementation decisions.[5]

Then, there is a disclaimer statement describing the intent of the IPS.

The investment policy statement is intended to communicate a philosophical approach to investing decisions. It is not, nor is it intended to be, a contract. It does not address legal responsibilities of either [you] or the Advisor, nor has it been reviewed or approved by an attorney. There is no guarantee that the goals identified in the investment policy statement will be achieved under the investment proposal prescribed.[6]

Client Summary

The client summary, which summarizes the underlying data collected in preparation of creating the IPS, is next.

[Your] needs and constraints are critical factors in developing an appropriate long-term investment approach. It is our goal to have a good understanding of your purpose in engaging our services, your financial goals, your tolerance for risk, and the level of assets to be applied in the proposal. We also strive to understand your need for liquidity, including the possibility that you may require access to invested assets over time. Finally, because investment decisions should take tax considerations into account, we seek information on tax constraints. The information below summarizes our understanding of your goals and current financial situation that will be considered in the investment proposal.[7]

---

5. Data sourced from © 2021 Morningstar, Inc. All Rights Reserved. Reproduced with permission. *Morningstar® Advisor Workstation*[SM] [Investment Policy Statement]. Retrieved January 2021.
6. *Id.*
7. *Id.*

Proposed Portfolio

The IPS then lays out a proposed portfolio, including a proposed asset allocation that reflects the expected risk and return behavior for your investments, an important factor in determining the specific securities. This is followed by how the portfolio is to be monitored.

Monitoring Statement

This is how Morningstar addresses how the adviser intends to monitor the portfolio.

> The investment proposal developed is intended to reflect a long-term approach, potentially lasting until goals are achieved. However, your financial situation and goals may change, producing a need to reconsider this plan. At the same time, financial markets are unpredictable in the short-term, producing temptation to recklessly deviate from a solid long-term plan. The goal of setting a portfolio monitoring agenda is to create flexibility for revising a strategy when needed, while providing structure to discourage overreaction to normal short-term market events.[8]

The IPS notes that asset allocations will be revisited based on an agreed upon time frequency between you and the investment adviser. Frequency should be tied to either the calendar or to a change in circumstances, such as retirement, marriage, the death of a spouse, or the addition or withdrawal of significant assets. It should also be updated for changes in investment goals.

Client Acceptance

Finally, there is an acceptance page that calls for you, the client, to specify that you read the IPS and that it accurately reflects your "personal needs and constraints and reflects an investment philosophy with which [you] feel comfortable."[9]

---

8. *Id.*
9. *Id.*

This is the basic structure of an IPS that you can expect an investment advisory firm to provide to you for discussion purposes. After discussing, the IPS serves as the plan for implementation and monitoring the portfolio.

Note: When presented with a draft IPS, take the opportunity to discuss it with your adviser before the IPS is finalized and implemented. It then serves as the basis for construction of your portfolio and your relationship with the firm. You should plan to revisit it periodically, especially when and if your needs change.

Key Takeaways

When retaining any type of financial firm, you, the client, need to be sure that the firm understands your situation well enough to craft a proposed portfolio to fit your circumstances. The firm needs to articulate how it will manage your portfolio. That can be a formal IPS or a conversation in less complicated situations.

If you retain an investment adviser to make investment decisions for you (discretionary portfolio management), you will want absolute clarity.

In such cases, if I put myself into the position of a client, I would want a written IPS to review in draft, to consider and discuss, to adjust as necessary, and to finalize. I would also want to review the IPS on a regular basis as warranted by changing circumstances or strategy. The IPS is an opportunity to understand the adviser's mission and to redirect efforts if the adviser is not in sync with you.

The next chapter explores how to put to use the concepts discussed in this chapter and Chapter 5 (cash flow analyses and methods to support portfolio withdrawals to fund living expenses).

Chapter 7
Setting Strategy Based on Three Situations and Goals

In this chapter, let's talk about three types of retirement situations that translate into retirement goals, based on personal cash flow. Think back to where you came out when you did your cash flow analysis in Chapter 5. Did you have a retirement income gap to fill?

Your answer will help you set your portfolio strategy, the topic of this chapter. First, we'll review your situation. Then, we'll see how to use that information to drive the most difficult of retirement portfolios to manage, those that require both filling a retirement income gap (Chapter 5) *and* creating a legacy. I'll share a top-level view of how I might organize such a portfolio following a method my firm calls "Demand-Driven." I will also introduce our term, "coverage ratio," a calculation we use to measure income production for any kind of portfolio, whether Demand-Driven or not.

Your Situation/Your Goals

When an adviser experienced in managing retirement portfolios prepares to set a strategy for a retirement portfolio, the most important question addressed is whether a retirement income gap needs to be filled. As a reminder, you have a retirement income gap if you need to withdraw money from your savings to help pay expenses in retirement. (A simple way to figure the dollar amount is to answer two questions: How much are you spending? How much Social Security and pension income (non-portfolio income) are you taking in? If your spending exceeds your non-portfolio income, you have a retirement income gap in the amount of the difference between the two figures.)

Consider the goals that flow from these three possibilities.

1. *No* retirement income gap. There is no need for regular portfolio withdrawals. Instead, the goal is to create or preserve capital, potentially leaving a legacy. This type of retirement portfolio is the easiest of all to structure and manage. In fact, this is the best situation to manage on your own if you are a self-directed investor who has a great interest in the financial markets. Be aware that if you are married, and your spouse does not share that interest, consider the risk to your spouse if you become incapacitated or pre-decease him or her.

2. Retirement income gap *without legacy interests*. The goal is to use savings to help pay bills for your lifetime (terminal value of zero). The management of this portfolio is more complicated than Goal 1, but much less complex than Goal 3, which follows. Complexity will depend on the capital involved, family structure, financial knowledge, interest, and horizon. If assets are modest, there may be product solutions that can be appropriate. If assets are significant, I would advise against trying to achieve Goal 2 on your own without outside expertise.

3. Retirement income gap *with legacy*. The goals are twofold: to create (1) income—a "paycheck" that lasts a lifetime, increasing over time to offset inflation and taxes, and (2) capital appreciation with the potential for a legacy for heirs or charity. This is the most difficult of all three scenarios, calling for the retention of an investment adviser skilled in this type of portfolio construction and management.

No Retirement Income Gap

In the first situation (Goal 1), you have *no need* for the portfolio to regularly produce cash flow. That leaves open a discussion about whether to grow or preserve savings. If growth is the goal, you could search for a different type of investment adviser than we've been discussing in this book, perhaps someone with expertise in:

- Beating the market (if you are not sensitive to market volatility)
- Targeting a chosen benchmark or index (if you like to judge results this way)

- Or even outperforming the past returns of another adviser (for those who see investing as a competitive sport)

Covering the Retirement Income Gap

For Goals 2 and 3, both of which have retirement income gaps, you will need expertise in creating cash flow for a lifetime.

Note: If you are interviewing a firm to manage your retirement portfolio, and that firm does not address cash flow needs with you before offering their services, the firm may not have retirement expertise. Consider interviewing another firm.

For Goal 3, the addition of a desired legacy adds a layer of complexity, calling for expertise in strategically structuring and managing portfolios to meet these goals. On your side of the equation are your investable assets, time horizon, tax situation, cash flow needs, family, and plans for the future. These factors will be important for determining the proper portfolio strategy and construction. On the firm's side of the equation, it will be important to discern the adviser's experience, skill, and methodology in meeting Goal 3 objectives. Not all advisers serve this need.

There are many ways to take on this challenge, the Demand-Driven process described next being one of them.

Demand-Driven Portfolio

The job of the Demand-Driven portfolio is to meet the "demands" placed on the portfolio by the client's desired cash flow to cover the retirement income gap and, at the same time, create capital appreciation for a future legacy. The demands "drive" the composition of the portfolio.

Such a portfolio is multifaceted. The objectives are to (1) accommodate planned after-tax withdrawals through income production *instead of selling holdings*; (2) anticipate withdrawals increasing over time (inflation, taxes, and extra expenses); (3) provide a cushion for unanticipated needs; (4) participate in the market for potential appreciation over time; (5) set a risk level for the overall portfolio *lower* than the broad market; (6) address the portfolio's time horizon; and (7) provide you with expectations for current income production, potential capital appreciation, and volatility to match your risk appetite and risk capacity.

Again, the starting point is the retirement income gap, which is produced through a cash flow sensitivity analysis (discussed in Chapter 5). Stock and bond allocations flow from that cash flow need.

Note: To use the Demand-Driven method, an individual's capital (savings) needs to support both cash flow needs and to provide for growth. When capital is insufficient, a review of investment goals leads to a different method of cash flow production, as discussed in Chapter 5.

Using the Demand-Driven method to construct a portfolio, our first consideration is how to deal with the withdrawals necessitated by the retirement income gap over the future retirement-legacy horizon (the length of which differs client to client). We weigh the strength of each portfolio methodology that can be utilized in light of each client's situation and goals, based on our cash flow and sensitivity analyses. Two critical elements dictate the structure: your time horizon and the capital available to commit to competing goals (income versus capital appreciation).

Using this process, we structure a portfolio to both fill your current retirement income gap and, at the same time, position the portfolio for future growth within appropriate risk parameters in order to meet future income and capital appreciation objectives, incorporating inflation and taxes into the equation.

That means your Investment Policy Statement (see Chapter 6) might have three objectives:

- The primary objective would be current income. That is, the portfolio would need to generate enough interest and dividend income to "cover" current withdrawals. We would measure this goal using "coverage ratio" as described later.
- The secondary objective would be long-term growth. That is, the portfolio would need to appreciate over time to offset inflation, taxes, new expenses, and possibly to provide a legacy for heirs.
- The tertiary objective would be to provide liquidity for taxes and out-of-sequence expenses and to support withdrawals, if need be, during down-market periods.

The IPS would include how progress would be monitored over time. One method of following cash flow is coverage ratio.

Introducing the "Coverage Ratio"

To periodically monitor the portfolio's income production against the client's withdrawals, we would use a measure we call "coverage ratio." While the use of the term coverage ratio in monitoring cash flow is our own (not industry) methodology, it is a useful measure that is easy enough to calculate. (Projected income divided by "annual need." Annual need is the dollar amount to be withdrawn from the portfolio to fill the retirement income gap, after taxes.) For example, in Table 7-1, the projected income of $200,000 is divided by the annual need of $120,000 to arrive at a coverage ratio of 1.67 (167 percent). A coverage ratio greater than 1, as in this example, means that the annual need is more than fully covered by the portfolio's projected annual income.

Table 7-1 Adequate Coverage Ratio

Annual Need	$120,000
Projected Annual Income	$200,000
Coverage Ratio	1.67

On the other hand, if the annual after-tax need is higher than the projected annual income, the coverage ratio will be below 1. In Table 7-2, our hypothetical retiree's annual need is $120,000, which is substantially higher than the projected annual income of $84,000. The coverage ratio is 0.7, which means that withdrawals are only 70 percent covered.

Table 7-2 Low Coverage Ratio

Annual Need	$120,000
Projected Annual Income	$84,000
Coverage Ratio	0.70

When capital is insufficient to cover withdrawals and to provide for capital appreciation at the same time, another cash flow method needs to be used. All will depend on the particular situation.

Note: No matter the cash flow method used by the adviser, coverage ratio can be a guide. When the coverage ratio is below 1, revisit (1) expenses (discretionary or essential), (2) allocations (stocks versus bonds), and (3) cash flow methodology.

Illustration

The best way to explain the Demand-Driven method is through an example. A widow, age 70, is withdrawing $120,000 a year from her portfolio to cover her retirement income gap, including her income tax bill. Her income (dividends and interest) production is $200,000 a year. Her withdrawals are "covered" by the income production. Her coverage ratio is over 1.0 (1.67 or $200,000 divided by $120,000), which means her withdrawals are supported by income production at this time, not principal.

The remainder of her portfolio is structured for long-term capital appreciation. In the future, withdrawals will need to increase due to inflation and to potentially support a legacy goal.

The initial allocations between growth and income are a function of current market conditions, time horizon, legacy expectations, and of course, risk. As one can imagine, since no one person's situation is like any other's, there is no one standard asset allocation that can be applied to all. Each portfolio is unique.

Who Can Use the Demand-Driven Process?

The Demand-Driven process is best used by high-net-worth families[1] whose assets are sufficient in size to support two objectives (income and capital appreciation) at the same time, even in low-interest-rate markets.

---

1. Advisers disclose the number of high-net-worth clients they serve in Form ADV. The term is defined in the SEC's Form ADV Instructions as a "qualified client." A qualified client is defined in Advisers Act rule 205-3 as an individual with at least $1.1 million in assets under management with the investment adviser immediately after entering into the advisory contract (or having a net worth in excess of $2.2 million). The number of high-net-worth individuals is an ADV disclosure item (5.D.) as is "other than high-net-worth individuals." ("Individuals" includes family members who are clients.) A different definition is used by wealth analysts, such as Wealth-X. Wealth-X divides "high-net-worth" into three levels: (1) "high-net-worth" is defined as net worth of $1 million to $5 million; (2) "very-high-net-worth" is $5 million to $30 million; (3) "ultra-high-net-worth" is $30 million and up. *World Ultra Wealth Report 2021*, Wealth-X.

This method would *not* be appropriate for families whose expected withdrawals are too high to be supported by the capital available to invest.

Key Takeaways

Retirees are not all alike. Some have retirement income gaps and some don't. Some have legacy goals and some don't. Before anyone can offer you advice on how to invest for your retirement, you need to know where you fall. Then you can determine how to proceed.

If you have a retirement income gap and a legacy goal, your situation is more complex to conceptualize and manage than others. The Demand-Driven process we discussed in this chapter is just one of many methods that can be useful in the right circumstances (sufficient capital considering portfolio demands). The methodology avoids the need to liquidate principal in order to generate cash flow for expenses while growing capital for the future. As a result, consider this method if you want your family to not only preserve lifestyle but also leave a legacy for children or charity or both.

In the next chapter, we'll talk about the types of reports that can help you follow the construction and performance of your portfolio.

Wealth-X is the global leader in wealth information and insight and produces global data analysis on wealthy individuals.

Chapter 8
Reports and Reviewing Progress

If I were a client looking for an investment adviser to structure and manage my retirement portfolio, I would want confirmation that the adviser and I are in sync. One way to do that is to carefully review a draft IPS (discussed in Chapter 6). The other is to ask to see the reports the adviser uses to monitor the portfolio and to report on progress.

You'll want the reports to answer the question: How am I doing? You'll need data to make that determination. What reports will you want to review? How will performance be judged? How will you know you're on track to meeting your goals?

In this chapter, we'll cover the kinds of reports your adviser might provide and how you might interpret them. We'll begin with brokerage statements, then, we'll turn to reports that can be helpful in monitoring progress to meet goals.

Custody

If you retain an investment adviser that is *independent* of a broker-dealer, expect (but confirm) that your assets will be held at a broker-dealer that acts as custodian[1] of your individual brokerage accounts. When the investment adviser onboards a new client, the adviser prepares account opening paperwork and transfer paperwork to engage the custodian to

---

1. According to RIA Biz 2020 list, https://riabiz.com/section/ria-custodians, the largest custodians are Schwab Advisor Services, Fidelity Institutional Wealth Services, State Street Wealth Manager Services, and Pershing Advisor Solutions, a subsidiary of BNY Mellon.

hold brokerage account assets and to execute brokerage transactions as directed by the investment adviser under a portfolio management (or supervisory) contract.

Brokerage Statements

The custodian's brokerage statements report the holdings and transactions in your brokerage accounts. If you are an investor, you're already familiar with brokerage statements. Brokerage statements usually show account holdings, values, and transactions, such as deposits, withdrawals, buys and sells, and dividends and interest earned. IRA account brokerage statements may also report required minimum distributions (RMDs). The brokerage statement and confirmations of transactions are mandated by the 1934 Act.

Investment Adviser Reports

Unlike brokerage statements that report transactions and positions that follow mandated requirements, investment advisers serving individual clients have flexibility in whether and how to report progress. As a result, how an adviser reports to a client can be a distinguishing characteristic when choosing an investment adviser to manage your retirement portfolio.

Information You Might Want to See

As someone with a focus on retirement, you'll want to see information that helps you understand your performance as measured by your objectives. If an objective is filling your retirement income gap, you'll want to see the methodology in place and how it is working. For example, in the last chapter, we discussed coverage ratio, which is a data point in my firm's reports. No matter the method used to produce portfolio withdrawals, you'll need a way to judge how they are being supported, whether by selling holdings, using cash set aside for withdrawals, through a product purchased to create income (an annuity), or through income produced by the portfolio, as we discussed in Chapter 5.

Another goal is capital appreciation, which can be assessed in a number of different ways, including benchmark comparisons. I like to see a portfolio's returns in the context of the risk assumed to achieve those returns. You would want to see how the portfolio held up in normal markets and under stress during down markets, such as during the COVID-19 bear market. You would also want to see results on a net after-fees-and-costs basis.

To give you an idea of possibilities, I'll share a series of reports my firm might use as part of a larger reporting package. *The samples are illustrations, not actual client reports.* We create these reports using portfolio management software, naming them as we see fit. As you read ahead, if you spot information that you would like your adviser to provide, more likely than not, it is available by request.

1. Allocation by Objective
2. Allocation Over Time by Objective
3. Performance by Objective
4. Holdings by Objective
5. Performance Evaluation
6. Index Returns

These reports can show data on a portfolio basis or the individual accounts that comprise the portfolio.

1. Allocation by Objective

To get a sense of asset allocation, we use a report called "Allocation by Objective." This report gives us a snapshot of allocations at a point in time.

In this example (see Figure 8-1), "Growth" is defined as capital appreciation instruments, such as stocks, stock mutual funds, and stock ETFs. "Income" is income-producing instruments such as bonds, whether they be corporate, municipal, high yield, or high quality. "Income & Growth" is a hybrid category (investments that hold both stocks and bonds). "Liquidity" is cash and cash equivalents. Any one of these objectives (even Growth) can include income-producing instruments that can create cash flow discussed in the last chapter. The allocation should reflect a structure designed to meet your objectives, risk tolerance, and constraints (such as a large holding with a low tax basis).

Figure 8-1 Allocation by Objective (Illustration)

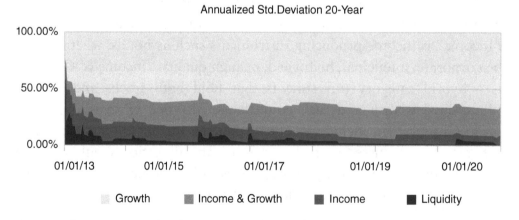

Source: Jackson, Grant. Produced using Orion Advisor Solutions.

2. Allocation Over Time by Objective

We also want to see different points in time for a historical view, especially in changing markets. The next graph (Figure 8-2) shows allocations over time, in this case, from 2013 through 2020.

Figure 8.2 shows you the flow of funds into different allocations over time. You can see that Growth and Income & Growth allocations increase slowly during portfolio construction, then stabilize over time. As mentioned before, allocations reflect your personal situation.

Figure 8-2 Allocation Over Time by Objective (Illustration)

Source: Jackson, Grant. Produced using Orion Advisor Solutions.

3. Performance by Objective

As a client of an investment adviser, I would want to understand the function of each allocation based on risk/reward and income/capital appreciation potential, particularly if I need my portfolio to support my lifestyle.

Note: The reports in this chapter are sample illustrations, not real data. The term "inception" would show the client's actual inception date.

The "Performance by Objective" report (Table 8-1) provides that information. It is my personal favorite, since it is most helpful in communicating the structure and objectives of the portfolio. Let me take you through this example; if you agree that it is helpful, ask your investment adviser to provide this data to you.

Table 8-1 Performance by Objective Since Inception to End Date (Illustration)

Category	End Date Value	Projected Annual Income	Current Yield	Projected Annual Need	Coverage Ratio	Beta Since Inception	Max Decline Since Inception	Annual Return Since Inception
Growth	$8,187,053	$117,930	1.0%			0.96	−52.0%	9.0%
Income & Growth	$3,211,025	$76,828	2.0%			0.63	−39.0%	7.0%
Income	$643,185	$22,978	4.0%			0.18	−13.0%	5.0%
Liquidity	$345,709	$0	0.0%			0.00	0.0%	1.0%
Total	$12,386,972	$217,736	2.0%	$120,000	1.8	0.53	−25.0%	7.0%

The End Date Value column reflects the category's value on that day. Projected Annual Income is the dollar value of the dividends and interest expected to be produced by the current holdings over the next 12 months. Current Yield is dividend and interest income as a percentage of dollar value. Projected Annual Need is the dollar amount that the client expects to withdraw from the portfolio for living expenses over the next 12 months. Coverage Ratio, discussed in Chapter 7, indicates whether the portfolio will fill your retirement income gap without having to sell principal—a value of 1 or more means that it is expected to fill the gap. (As a reminder, Coverage Ratio equals projected annual income divided by projected annual need.)

The portfolio's risk is measured in two ways: Beta and Max Decline.

Beta, discussed in Chapter 4, is a construct that measures the sensitivity of the portfolio to the movements of a benchmark, such as the S&P 500 Index.[2] Beta is backward looking; you normally want to see 36 months of data before drawing conclusions (for statistical significance).

A portfolio with a Beta lower than 1 indicates less stock market risk (and less potential reward) than the S&P 500 Index over time. A portfolio with a Beta higher than 1 indicates higher risk and higher potential return than the S&P 500 Index. In retirement, I would want a portfolio Beta of less than 1 in most cases.

Max Decline shows how much the portfolio declined during the worst of times since the portfolio's inception. Max Decline is the percentage peak to trough decline during the reported period. It is not a withdrawal, and it is not a realized loss—it's simply the temporary price decline actually experienced.

This measure of volatility helps one understand structure, leading to a conversation between the client and the investment adviser to either accept or change the composition of the portfolio based on risk and potential reward.

Take a moment to compare the Growth Objective to the Income Objective. You'll see that the Growth Objective is much more volatile just by looking at the Max Decline. Keep in mind that the period in this illustration included three bear markets, the bursting of the Internet Bubble, the Financial Crisis, and the coronavirus bear. You'll also see that the return for the Growth Objective was also the highest, reflecting three bull markets in between the three bears.

The Growth Objective's Max Decline was the deepest (−52 percent) with the highest Annual Return (9 percent); followed by the Max Decline for Income and Growth of −39 percent with an Annual Return of 7 percent. Then, came Income with a Max Decline of −13 percent and an Annual Return of 5 percent, followed by a Max Decline of zero for Liquidity and an Annual Return of 1 percent. These results are consistent with risk and reward expectations over time.

---

2. Be aware that not all data sources measure Beta against the S&P 500. Be sure to check.

This is an important set of data points to make sure you and your adviser agree on the allocation made to each asset class, with an understanding of the risk-reward trade-offs for each.

4. Holdings by Objective

A "Holdings by Objective" report shows individual holdings for an account or a household. The following report (see Table 8-2) shows positions sorted by objective, then by weight (percentage of the portfolio), with the highest weight at the top. End Date Value is self-explanatory. Projected Annual Income is interest and dividends expected for each security, as well as the total for the account or household. The Current Yield is the annual income divided by the current value of the security for the portfolio or household. Net Return Annual Since Inception is the total return, annualized, net of fees. Unrealized Gain/Loss is the dollar difference between the current value and the cost basis.

Table 8-2 Holding Returns for Period Since Inception to End Date (Illustration)

Objective	Weight	Holding*	End Date Value	Projected Annual Income	Current Yield	Net Return Annual Since Inception	Unrealized Gain/Loss
Growth	3.4%	Security A	$427,036	$2,803	0.70%	17.60%	$316,813
	3.1%	Security B	$382,591	$3,853	1.00%	27.30%	$315,962
	2.7%	Security C	$337,183	$5,132	1.50%	14.80%	$207,344
	***		***	***	***	***	***
Income & Growth	4.5%	Security D	$553,933	$9,160	1.70%	9.90%	$235,244
	1.8%	Security E	$224,886	$7,861	3.50%	5.20%	$51,749
	1.1%	Security F	$134,374	$2,889	2.10%	9.50%	$34,324
	***		***	***	***	***	***
Income	2.2%	Security G	$270,402	$5,792	2.10%	5.90%	$24,727
	1.8%	Security H	$228,439	$10,382	4.50%	8.20%	$17,573
	1.2%	Security I	$144,344	$6,679	4.60%	7.00%	$8,714
	***		***	***	***	***	***
Liquidity	1.2%	Cash	$144,344				
Total	100%		***	***	***	***	***

*While Table 8-2 anonymizes holdings, the client's report specifies the holding and symbol.

With this type of report, you can zero in on the individual holdings that fall into the objective. That alignment helps one understand the contribution of the holding to the overall goals of the portfolio. The report can also open up a conversation with your adviser about performance detractors and contributors.

5. Performance Evaluation

A "Performance Evaluation" report (see Table 8-3) looks at different time periods, in this case, the most recent quarter-to-date (Last Quarter), the last calendar year (Last Year), and Since Inception. This report is intended to give you a sense of both money movement (contributions you made to the portfolio and the withdrawals you have taken out of the portfolio) and results (dividends and interest and capital appreciation after fees are deducted).

The data points are:

- Beginning Market Value. This is the dollar amount that you started with at the beginning of each period.
- Contributions/Withdrawals. Contributions are cash (or the value of securities) you deposited during the relevant period. Withdrawals are cash or securities withdrawn from the portfolio. (Net contributions gives you the difference between contributions and withdrawals.)
- Dividends & Interest. Dividends and interest are dollars generated from securities (generally stock dividends and bond interest payments) during the period, including those reinvested.
- Capital Appreciation (After Fees). This dollar amount shows the increase or decrease due to changes in prices of the holdings for the period shown, reduced by advisory fees.
- Ending Market Value. The ending market value shows a dollar value of the portfolio at the point in time shown in the report.
- Net Gain/Loss. This is the amount that the portfolio earned during the period, which is calculated by adding together dividends and interest earned and capital appreciation (after fees are deducted).
- Net Time Weighted Return. This translates Net Gain/Loss into a percentage annualized return. The return is reported as "Time Weighted"[3]

---

3. Carl R. Bacon, CIPM, David R. Cariño, PhD, & Arin Stancil, CFA, CIPM, CFA Reading 4, Performance Evaluation: Rate-of-Return Measurement 265–66 (CFA Inst. 2019),

Table 8-3 Performance Evaluation for Periods Shown (Illustration)

Portfolio Returns for Period			
	Last Quarter	**Last Year**	**Since Inception (over 20 years)**
Beginning Market Value	$11,195,333	$10,924,485	$0
Contributions	$0	$0	$4,792,695
Withdrawals	($12,457)	($256,489)	($2,592,275)
Net Contributions (Contributions/ Withdrawals)	($12,457)	($256,489)	$2,200,419
Dividends & Interest	$61,903	$222,986	$3,442,140
Capital Appreciation (After Fees)	$1,142,194	$1,495,991	$6,744,413
Ending Market Value	$12,386,973	$12,386,973	$12,386,973
Net Gain/Loss	$1,204,097	$1,718,977	$10,186,553
Net Time Weighted Return (TWR) for Portfolio	11%	16%	7%

in order to match the standard for reporting benchmark returns. Another way to report is using "Dollar Weighted Return" (also called Internal Rate of Return, or IRR), which includes the investor's cash flows (deposits and withdrawals).

The report shows money movement in and out of the portfolio ("contributions" and "withdrawals") as well as results broken down by income and capital appreciation, gains or losses, and returns for different time frames. Index returns are shown in the next report.

6. Index Returns

An "Index Returns" report sets out an array of index returns that can be used by an investor to compare individual holdings or the portfolio as a whole. However, beware of the potential traps of using index data to *judge* a portfolio, as we will discuss shortly. Let's review the report first.

https://www.cfainstitute.org/-/media/documents/support/programs/cipm/2019-cipm-l1v1r4.ashx.

The following report (see Table 8-4) shows returns for a selection of common indices. TR stands for total return, which includes price change plus dividends, if any.

Table 8-4 Index Returns for Periods Shown (Illustration)

	Last Quarter	Last Year	Since Inception (over 20 years)
Barclays Aggregate Bond (TR)	1%	8%	5%
60% Morningstar Dividend Leaders/ 35%BCAgg/5%TBill (TR)	9%	2%	7%
Morningstar Dividend Leaders (TR)	15%	–4%	8%
S&P 500 Equal Weighted (TR)	19%	13%	10%
S&P 500 Market Cap Weighted (TR)	12%	18%	9%

Some indices are for fixed-income instruments (Barclays Aggregate Bond Index of U.S. Investment Grade Bonds). Other indices are 100 percent stock indices (S&P 500 Index Total Return) or less, such as "60% Morningstar Dividend Leaders; 35% Barclays Agg; plus 5% T-Bill." The "Morningstar Dividend Leaders Benchmark" represents an index comprised of 100 stocks, chosen for dividend sustainability and consistency.

There are two S&P 500 indices shown. The S&P 500 index (S&P 500 Index Market Cap Weighted) is a market capitalization weighted index, which is the most widely used index to track the broad stock market. (Market capitalization is a way to measure the "market value" of a corporation at a point in time by multiplying the total number of outstanding shares by the current price of one share of the corporation.) A market capitalization weighted index holds each stock in proportion to its total market value; that is, larger companies make up a larger portion of the index. The second S&P 500 Index (S&P 500 Equal Weighted) shown is an S&P 500 Index that holds the 500 stocks in equal proportion instead of by capitalization.

Note: To be useful, you have to be aware of what indices represent. For example, in 2020, we experienced a dramatic divergence between dividend-paying stocks and non-dividend-paying growth stocks. From the beginning of 2020 to June 30, 2020, the S&P 500

Index (market cap weighted), which was dominated by large tech stocks, was down 3.1 percent, while dividend-producing stocks (represented by the Morningstar Dividend Leaders Index) lost substantially more (19.7 percent). This type of divergence in stock index returns is notable. When an index reflects unusual market movements, your investment adviser should explain the fluctuations to make sure you understand the significance of the market movements for your portfolio.

When Are Indices Useful/Not Useful?

There are circumstances that can call for an adviser to set a target for a portfolio. For example, assuming you have *no* retirement income gap, your objective could be solely capital appreciation (total return). Your adviser could target the S&P 500 Index (either cap weighted or equal weighted, depending on the situation). The goal would be to meet or beat the S&P 500 Index. That's the perfect scenario to use indices to judge portfolio performance.

If the goal is *anything other than a targeted return*, as would be the case with retirement portfolios for people who *do* have retirement income gaps, the S&P 500 Index would be a harmful distraction. To put it another way, when the objective is a retirement portfolio that creates income, *the S&P 500 Index is the wrong measure*.

Note: Beware of potential traps in using an index to judge a retirement portfolio that is not managed to match a target index.

That is, (1) index returns do not reflect the composition of a retirement portfolio (no customization to match your risk tolerance; no cash flow measures); and (2) no one index is likely to encompass the composition of the portfolio, although a blend may be close. To address the latter point, there are software programs that calculate a "dynamic benchmark" to assign indices to holdings as portfolio composition changes day to day. However even these benchmarks do not address risk tolerance and cash flow needs, which are the key determinants of performance for a retirement portfolio. It's the investment adviser's job to give you context.

Best Metrics

The metrics used to judge how your portfolio is doing have to align with your objectives (again, refer to Chapter 7). To make sure they do, talk to your investment adviser. Make sure you are in sync with your adviser on appropriate metrics.

Key Takeaways

Reports provided to clients differ from firm to firm; there is no mandated reporting requirement. You will want your investment adviser to report to you in a way that enhances your understanding of how the adviser is meeting your investment objectives and executing your investment policy. Reports will help you understand how your portfolio is performing, so that you can engage in a conversation with your adviser about meeting your goals for cash flow and capital appreciation, considering your time horizon and risk profile.

Consider the following:

- Are your reports helping you understand the methodology being used by the firm to meet your objectives?
- Are you getting confirmation that you are on track to meeting your needs?
- Are your reports helping you see how the firm is monitoring progress toward your goals?
- Do you need additional reporting or information that can assist you in the effort of understanding how your portfolio is being managed?

Ideally, reports enhance your understanding of how your portfolio is structured to meet your investment objectives and how it is performing relative to expectations. Reports will also help you dialogue with your investment adviser, as you address any changes necessitated by new cash flow needs or other changes in your investment goals.

PART III
New Due Diligence Tools Help You Make Informed Decisions

When introducing personal portfolio management in Part I of the book, we talked about the circumstances under which you might want to retain expertise to manage your retirement portfolio and when you might want to manage it yourself.

In Part II, we discussed how the personal portfolio management function might work, including methods of producing cash flow, how to design a portfolio to create cash flow, how to set policy, and how to measure progress.

The goal of Part III of the book is to introduce you to momentous regulatory changes that now provide investors with information that was very difficult for them to obtain easily on their own. Having that ability now will help you understand service offerings in a way that will give you context beyond marketing and sales materials. The key document is the new two- (or four-) page disclosure called "Form CRS," which is now required of broker-dealers, investment advisers, and dual registrants.

To give you a frame of reference, we'll start with the big picture, focusing on firms regulated by the SEC (Chapter 9, Financial Firms: Who's Who and What to Expect as a Client). Then, we'll address standards of care (Chapter 10, Do Standards of Care Matter? Should They?), followed by conflicts imbedded in the financial services industry, and how they differ from firm to firm (Chapter 11, Expect to Experience Conflicts of Interest, But Choose Not To). In that last chapter, we'll also address the question: Is there such a thing as a conflict-free firm?

Chapter 12 is about the CRS itself (Chapter 12, Form CRS Is Key). Chapter 13, Let's Talk: The SEC's "Conversation Starters" and More, presents questions to pose to representatives of investment advisers and broker-dealers.

This part of the book will help you discern the significant differences that exist between firms and their service models—all in preparation for you to choose the services best suited to your situation.

Chapter 9
Financial Firms: Who's Who and What to Expect as a Client

Regulators and investor advocates believe consumers lack clarity when it comes to understanding who's who in financial services. All agree that this needs to be rectified. It is vitally important for investors to know the playing field of financial firms and their representatives. The reason is simple: to avoid miscues. It seems that everyone is a "financial *adviser*" and potentially a "*fiduciary*." That is simply not the case. Thinking so can result in hiring the wrong type of firm based on a lack of awareness of services, fees, and most importantly, standards of care.

In this chapter, you'll get an introduction to the regulatory landscape along with resources for further study. The goal is to start getting a feel for criteria that you will find important when deciding on the type of firm you want to work with in retirement.

Note: Using the term "adviser" is now limited to representatives who are regulated under the Investment Advisers Act of 1940 (the "Advisers Act").[1]

---

1. Regulations no longer permit financial representatives to call themselves financial "advisers" unless they are regulated under the Investment Advisers Act of 1940 (the "Advisers Act"). Regulation Best Interest: The Broker-Dealer Standard of Conduct, U.S. Sec. & Exch. Comm'n, 17 C.F.R. § 240 (2019) 157–58, https://www.sec.gov/rules/final /2019/34-86031.pdf. Effective Sept. 10, 2019.

Regulation

As we discussed briefly in Chapter 1, the SEC regulates financial service providers based on their business models under two separate statutes: the Investment Advisers Act of 1940 (the "Advisers Act"), governing the giving of investment advice, and the Securities Exchange Act of 1934 (the "1934 Act"), governing investment transactions.

While there are two statutes, there are three types of firms registered under these acts:

1. Investment advisers ("stand-alone advisers")
2. Broker-dealers ("stand-alone broker-dealers")
3. "Dual registrants" (firms that do business as both investment advisers and broker-dealers)

Does regulation matter to you as an individual investor? The SEC thinks it should.

Investor Confusion? Seeking Clarity

According to the SEC, "Studies have shown that retail investors are confused about the differences among financial service providers, such as broker-dealers, investment advisers, and dual-registrants."[2]

To offer investors clarity, this is how I see the SEC addressing the problem.

First, you have needs:

Individual investors rely on the services of broker-dealers and investment advisers when making and implementing investment decisions.[3]

---

2. Regulation Best Interest Proposed Rule at https://www.sec.gov/rules/proposed /2018/34-83062.pdf. *See also* Form CRS Proposed Rule at https://www.sec.gov/rules /proposed/2018/34-83063.pdf. *See* footnote 5 noting CFA 2010 Survey; *see also* Siegel & Gale, LLC/Gelb Consulting Group, Inc., Results of Investor Focus Group Interviews About Proposed Brokerage Account Disclosures (Mar. 5, 2005), http://www.sec.gov /rules/proposed/s72599/focusgrp031005.pdf ("Siegel & Gale Study"); Angela A. Hung et al., RAND Institute for Civil Justice, Investor and Industry Perspectives on Investment Advisers and Broker-Dealers (2008), https://www.sec.gov/news/press/2008/2008-1_rand iabdreport.pdf ("RAND Study").

3. Form CRS Relationship Summary; Amendments to Form ADV; Required Disclosures in Retails Communications and Restrictions on the Use of Certain Names or

Second, you have choices:

Such "retail investors" can receive investment advice from a broker-dealer, an investment adviser, or both, or decide to make their own investment decisions. A number of firms are dually registered with the Commission as broker-dealers and investment advisers, and offer both types of services.[4]

Third, the choices are confusing:

Broker-dealers, investment advisers and dually registered firms all provide important services for individuals who invest in the markets. Studies show that retail investors are confused about the differences among them.[5]

Fourth, the choices are confusing for good reason:

These differences include the scope and nature of the services they provide, the fees and costs associated with those services, conflicts of interest, and the applicable legal standards and duties to investors.[6]

Fifth, nonetheless, there *are* benefits to having choices:

We recognize the benefits of retail investors having access to diverse business models and of preserving investor choice among brokerage services, advisory services, or both.[7]

Sixth, we need to make sure investors have clarity so that they can make informed choices:

We also believe that retail investors need clear and sufficient information in order to understand the differences and key characteristics of each type of service.[8]

Titles, U.S. Sec. & Exch. Comm'n, 17 C.F.R. § 200, 240, 249, 275, 279 (2019) 7, https://www.sec.gov/rules/proposed/2018/34-83063.pdf.
  4. *Id.*
  5. *Id.*
  6. *Id.* at 8.
  7. *Id.*
  8. *Id.*

Seventh, clarity is important so that you can get the service that is right for you:

> *Providing this clarity is intended to assist investors in making an informed choice when choosing an investment firm and professional, and type of account to help to ensure they receive services that meet their needs and expectations.*[9]

Does it matter to individual investors to be able to select the firm that meets their needs and expectations? I think you will agree that it does. The question is, how does one get clarity?

The SEC Delivers

After many years of study, the SEC issued a series of regulatory actions in 2019 to help consumers distinguish between firms, their services, and the legal standards of care that apply. This important rulemaking reaffirmed investment advisers' fiduciary duty. For broker-dealers, it introduced new disclosure obligations and raised the standard of conduct. For both broker-dealers and investment advisers, the SEC created a new disclosure document (the Client Relationship Summary, or CRS). (We will discuss these developments further in later chapters from the point of view of the retiree who needs to retain expertise for retirement investing.)

The SEC didn't spare any paper, which indicates the complexity of the regulation of financial service providers. I'll provide you with a short history. If you want to better understand the nature of the industry, the releases mentioned next are well worth your time, for your own knowledge, and more so, if you make referrals to financial service providers or act as a fiduciary.

The SEC's Four 2019 Releases

The SEC issued four important releases on June 5, 2019, highlighting rulemaking that had been in the works for decades. The SEC had a lot to say about the topic of who's who on Wall Street and why Main Street investors like you and your clients should care.

---

9. *Id.*

1. "Regulation Best Interest: The Broker-Dealer Standard of Care" (770-page, final rule).[10] This important release introduces a stronger standard of care for broker-dealers and dual registrants ("Best Interest") along with new disclosures, and includes a detailed review of the suitability standard of care.[11] The release also points out that broker-dealers should not present themselves as investment advisers. A complication arises when a dual registrant's registered representatives act in the capacity of supervised persons of an investment adviser, in which case it is appropriate to use the nomenclature when acting as an investment adviser representative of the firm. Compliance with Regulation Best Interest was required by June 30, 2020. We will discuss the best interest standard for brokers and dual registrants in the next chapter.

2. "Form CRS Relationship Summary; Amendments to Form ADV" (564-page, final rule).[12] The CRS is a new mandated disclosure that must be provided to retail investors (beginning in 2020) by broker-dealers, investment advisers, and dual registrants. The document is limited to two pages if the firm is a stand-alone adviser or a stand-alone broker-dealer. A dual registrant is limited to four pages. The CRS is the key document for searching for an appropriate firm to retain. We will review the CRS in Chapter 12.

3. "Commission Interpretation Regarding Standard of Conduct for Investment Advisers"[13] (42 pages). This release confirms that

---

10. Regulation Best Interest: The Broker-Dealer Standard of Conduct, *supra* note 1.

11. Note that FINRA amended its suitability rule in June 2020 to conform to the best interest standard. See Regulatory Notice 20-18, "Reg BI-Related Changes to FINRA Rules." FINRA (the Financial Industry Regulatory Authority) is a not-for-profit, self-regulatory organization (SRO) responsible for regulating its member broker-dealers and their associated persons pursuant to the 1934 Act. https://www.finra.org/sites/default/files /2020-06/Regulatory-Notice-20-18.pdf, © 2020 FINRA. All rights reserved. FINRA is a registered trademark of the Financial Industry Regulatory Authority, Inc. Reprinted with permission from FINRA.

12. Form CRS Relationship Summary; Amendments to Form ADV, U.S. Securities and Exchange Commission, 17 C.F.R. § 200, 240, 249, 275, 279. (2019). https://www .sec.gov/rules/final/2019/34-86032.pdf.

13. Commission Interpretation Regarding Standard of Conduct for Investment Advisers, U.S. Securities and Exchange Commission, 17 C.F.R. § 276 (2019), https:// www.sec.gov/rules/interp/2019/ia-5248.pdf. Effective July 12, 2019.

investment advisers are held to the higher fiduciary duty. We will discuss the fiduciary standard in the next chapter.

4. "Commission Interpretation Regarding the Solely Incidental Prong of the Broker-Dealer Exclusion from the Definition of Investment Adviser"[14] (28 pages). This release addresses the limited circumstances under which a broker-dealer that provides certain types of investment advice can avoid registering as an investment adviser.

The SEC's Three 2018 Releases

This rulemaking followed earlier proposals from April 18, 2018. These 2018 releases show the thinking, research, and survey data that went behind the final adoption of rules in 2019, including focus group studies of investors.

1. Form CRS Relationship Summary; Amendments to Form ADV; Required Disclosures in Retail Communications and Restrictions on the Use of Certain Names or Titles (471-page, proposed rule).[15] This release proposed Form CRS and should be read if one wants a nuanced understanding of the need for such disclosure. The release also discusses survey data about confusion on the part of investors in distinguishing services of broker-dealers, advisers, and dual registrants.

2. Regulation Best Interest (408-page, proposed rule).[16] This release establishes the arguments for a new standard of care for brokers called Best Interest.

---

14. Commission Interpretation Regarding the Solely Incidental Prong of the Broker-Dealer Exclusion from the Definition of Investment Adviser, U.S. Securities and Exchange Commission, 17 C.F.R. § 276 (2019), https://www.sec.gov/rules/interp/2019/ia-5249.pdf. Effective July 12, 2019.

15. Form CRS Relationship Summary; Amendments to Form ADV; Required Disclosures in Retails Communications and Restrictions on the use of Certain Names or Titles, U.S. Securities and Exchange Commission, 17 C.F.R. § 200, 240, 249, 275, 279 (2019), https://www.sec.gov/rules/proposed/2018/34-83063.pdf.

16. Regulation Best Interest, U.S. Securities and Exchange Commission, 17 C.F.R. § 240 (2018), https://www.sec.gov/rules/proposed/2018/34-83062.pdf.

3. Proposed Commission Interpretation Regarding Standard of Conduct for Investment Advisers; Request for Comment on Enhancing Investment Adviser Regulation[17] (38 pages). This release focuses on adviser responsibility.

Note: The 2018 releases triggered thousands of comment letters on both the Best Interest proposal[18] and the CRS proposal,[19] including comments from this author.[20] The volume of commentary says something; clearly, these are important topics for both the industry and the individual investors who took the time to express their views.

You Have Choices Based on Your Needs

How can you distinguish between broker-dealers and investment advisers? Through these regulations, the SEC offers a way: "As a general matter, broker-dealers and investment advisers have different types of *relationships* with investors, offer different *services*, and have different *compensation* models when providing investment recommendations or investment advisory services to customers."[21]

Investment advisers "typically provide ongoing, regular advice and services in the context of broad investment portfolio management and are compensated based on the value of assets under management (AUM),

---

17. Proposed Commission Interpretation Regarding Standard of Conduct for Investment Advisers; Request for Comment on Enhancing Investment Adviser Regulation, 17 C.F.R. § 276 (2018), https://www.sec.gov/rules/proposed/2018/ia-4889.pdf.

18. Comments on Proposed Rule: Regulation Best Interest, U.S Securities and Exchange Commission, sec.gov, (last modified May 21, 2021), https://www.sec.gov/comments/s7-07-18/s70718.htm.

19. Comments on Form CRS Relationship Summary; Amendments to Form ADV; Required Disclosures in Retail Communications and Restrictions on the Use of Certain Names or Titles, https://www.sec.gov/comments/s7-08-18/s70818.htm.

20. https://www.sec.gov/comments/s7-08-18/s70818-4239609-173000.pdf.

21. Regulation Best Interest: The Broker-Dealer Standard of Conduct, *supra* note 10, at 6-7 (emphasis added).

a fixed fee or other arrangement ('fee-based' compensation or model)."[22] Note the reference to *portfolio management* and *ongoing, regular advice.* (See Chapter 1 for a discussion of personal portfolio management.)

In contrast, broker-dealers provide "transaction-specific recommendations" for which brokers "receive compensation on a transaction-by-transaction basis (such as commissions) ('transaction-based' compensation or model)."[23] This would be the type of service you would want if you decided to manage your own retirement portfolio without an investment adviser.

Where does this leave you, the retail investor? Again, with choices. In the SEC's words, this taxonomy "presents investors with choices regarding the types of relationships they can have, the services they can receive, and how they can pay for those services."[24]

The Playing Field

Given that the SEC's rulemaking goal is designed to help investors "better understand and compare the services offered by broker-dealers and investment advisers,"[25] it's a worthwhile effort for investors to understand the regulations. Those regulations are meant to "provide clarity with respect to the standards of conduct applicable to investment advisers and broker-dealers, and foster greater consistency in the level of protections provided by each regime, particularly at the point in time that a recommendation is made."[26]

The SEC's ultimate goal, after all, is for investors to be able to "make an informed choice of the relationship best suited to their needs and circumstances."[27]

---

22. Regulation Best Interest: The Broker-Dealer Standard of Conduct," *supra* note 10, at 7.

23. *Id.*

24. *Id.*

25. Regulation Best Interest: The Broker-Dealer Standard of Conduct, *supra* note 10, at 16.

26. *Id.*

27. *Id.*

In the mix are nearly 13,000[28] stand-alone investment advisers registered with the SEC. The majority are small businesses. Nearly nine out of ten have 50 or fewer employees; 58.2 percent have ten or fewer employees.[29] The SEC publishes a list of SEC-registered advisers, which the SEC updates monthly.[30]

Even though there are only about 500 dual registrant firms (registered as both broker-dealers and investment advisers),[31] one out of two brokers (about 300,000 of 600,000 registered representatives) works for these large firms.[32] These dual registrants hold over 90 million (64 percent) of the overall 140 million customer accounts held by broker-dealers.[33] FINRA publishes a list of broker-dealers, which is updated monthly.[34]

---

28. Regulation Best Interest: The Broker-Dealer Standard of Conduct, *supra* note 10, at 413. "More than 2,600 (about 20 percent) of these advisers have an affiliated broker-dealer, representing approximately 74 percent of the total assets under management by SEC registered advisers." *See* Commission Interpretation Regarding the Solely Incidental Prong of the Broker-Dealer Exclusion from the Definition of Investment Adviser (2019). 2018 data. Footnote 76 at 23, https://www.sec.gov/rules/interp/2019/ia-5249.pdf.

29. *See* Investment Adviser Association (IAA) report, "Investment Adviser Industry Snapshot 2021" https://higherlogicdownload.s3.amazonaws.com/INVESTMENTADVI SER/aa03843e-7981-46b2-aa49-c572f2ddb7e8/UploadedImages/publications/industry -snapshots/Investment_Adviser_Industry_Snapshot_2021.pdf and online data link on page 16.

30. For a list of SEC advisers that is updated monthly, see SEC Bulletin, Information about Registered Investment Advisers and Exempt Reporting Advisers, https://www.sec .gov/help/foiadocsinvafoiahtm.html.

31. 2021 FINRA Industry Snapshot. 2021 Industry Snapshot. FINRA, May 2021. Data as of 12/31/2020, https://www.finra.org/sites/default/files/2021-06/21_0078.1 _Industry_Snapshot_v8.pdf, at 13. © 2021 FINRA. All rights reserved. FINRA is a registered trademark of the Financial Industry Regulatory Authority, Inc. Reprinted with permission from FINRA.

32. *Id.* There are roughly 600,000 registered representatives who work for broker-dealers. About 2,900 stand-alone broker-dealers employ about 300,000 registered representatives; the rest are employed by 300 dual registrants.

33. "Commission Interpretation Regarding the Solely Incidental Prong of the Broker-Dealer Exclusion from the Definition of Investment Adviser" (2019). 2018 data at 22, https://www.sec.gov/rules/interp/2019/ia-5249.pdf.

34. FINRA's list of broker-dealers is at https://www.finra.org/about/firms-we-regu late/broker-dealer-firms-we-regulate. © 2021 FINRA. All rights reserved. FINRA is a registered trademark of the Financial Industry Regulatory Authority, Inc. Reprinted with permission from FINRA.

Key Takeaways

Investors have been known to be confused about financial service providers, rightly so, since titles and services seem to be similar. With the goal of protecting investors, the SEC adopted regulations that gave firms guidance on how to interact with investors and also provided tools for investors to clarify differences between firms.

Considering these regulatory changes, investors have a bit of a learning curve to overcome to fully appreciate how to benefit from the new regulatory environment. However, the task at hand is not overwhelming by any means, as the keystone is a new disclosure document that is a mere two (or four) pages long, Form CRS.

Form CRS will help you understand how firms differ in what really matters: services, standards of care, conflicts of interest, disciplinary matters, and other distinctions. Reviewing the CRS will help you visualize what it's like to be a retirement client of the firm you are currently working with or a potential client of a firm new to you. Before we jump into the CRS, we need some context.

Let's review standards of care (next chapter) and then conflicts of interest (Chapter 11).

Chapter 10
Do Standards of Care Matter? Should They?

Should the fact that different standards of care apply to different firms matter to you? Should it make a difference to retirees who at some point in their lives, may want to be less involved with driving investment decisions, or worse, become unable to do so due to incapacity?

This chapter will help you understand the differences in business models that lead to different standards of care.

Should the Standard Be the Same for Brokers and Advisers?

As someone with both broker-dealer and investment adviser experience, I believe that consumers need commissioned salesmen to execute trades just as much as they need fiduciary investment advisers to manage retirement portfolios. Despite the different roles, some influential backers of the fiduciary standard[1] would rather see all financial services providers subject to the higher fiduciary standard.

The SEC did consider raising broker-dealer standards to fiduciary and rejected that approach for good reason. In its rulemaking, the SEC noted that "[a]dopting a 'one size fits all' approach would risk reducing investor *choice* and access to existing products, services, service providers, and

---

1. For example, Rep. Maxine Waters, chair of the Financial Services Committee, has stated that she would like to abolish the Best Interest Rule and replace it with a fiduciary rule for brokers. *See* Joseph Calabrese, *Maxine Waters Presses Biden to Rescind Reg BI*, JDSupra (Jan. 5, 2021), https://www.jdsupra.com/legalnews/maxine-waters-presses -biden-to-rescind-4129063/.

payment options, and would increase costs for firms and for retail inves-tors in both broker-dealer and investment adviser relationships."[2]

That's the key to understanding these regulations. The SEC is clarify-ing what you need to know about service providers in order to give you choices. *The challenge for you is to get clarity on those choices.*

A foundational concept is the regulatory standard of care that distin-guishes broker-dealers from investment advisers. In its best interest rule-making, the SEC affirmed the fiduciary standard for investment advisers and established a new standard of care for brokers, called "best interest," which was meant to augment, not displace the historic "suitability" stan-dard.[3] Subsequently, FINRA amended its suitability rule to clarify that the suitability rule does not apply to recommendations that are subject to Regulation Best Interest.[4]

Note: Both broker-dealers and investment advisers must act in the best interest of the customer; however, a broker's responsibilities are satisfied at the time of the recommendation, the point of sale, while the investment adviser's responsibilities continue for the length of the advisory relationship.

---

2. Regulation Best Interest: The Broker-Dealer Standard of Conduct, U.S. Sec. & Exch. Comm'n, 17 C.F.R § 240 (2019) 20, https://www.sec.gov/rules/final/2019/34-86031.pdf. Effective Sept. 10, 2019 (emphasis added).

3. "Regulation Best Interest will enhance the broker-dealer standard of conduct beyond existing suitability obligations and make it clear that a broker-dealer may not put its financial interests ahead of the interests of a retail customer when making rec-ommendations." June 5, 2019, release, "The SEC Adopts Rules and Interpretations to Enhance Protection and Preserve Choice For Retail Investors in Their Relationships with Financial Professionals."

Suitability is governed by FINRA rule 2111. The rule requires brokers to have "a reasonable basis to believe that a recommended transaction or investment strategy involving a security or securities is suitable for the customer, based on the information obtained through the reasonable diligence of the [firm] or associated person to ascertain the customer's investment profile." Suitability is discussed in detail in the "Regulation Best Interest: The Broker-Dealer Standard of Conduct," https://www.sec.gov/rules/final/2019/34-86031.pdf.

4. See FINRA Regulatory Notice 20-18 "Reg BI-Related Changes to FINRA Rules" at https://www.finra.org/sites/default/files/2020-06/Regulatory-Notice-20-18.pdf. © 2021 FINRA. All rights reserved. FINRA is a registered trademark of the Financial Industry Regulatory Authority, Inc. Reprinted with permission from FINRA.

From a practical point of view, you want brokerage services to be discrete and tied to the execution of the transaction—that's the service an investor signs up for. You want the investment adviser to maintain watch over the portfolio over time as the portfolio and the client's situation evolve—that's the service contracted, and that's the service that is governed by the long-standing fiduciary standard of care, which the SEC affirmed in its June 2019 release[5] to be the standard that applied to investment advisers.

Let's review the adviser's standard of care first, then the broker-dealer's.

The Fiduciary Standard of Care for Investment Advisers

The fiduciary standard is a long-standing, well-established principle set in 1963 by the U.S. Supreme Court in *SEC v. Capital Gains Research Bureau, Inc.*[6]

Fiduciary duty "reflects a Congressional recognition 'of the delicate fiduciary nature of an investment advisory relationship'" as well as a congressional intent to "eliminate, or at least to expose, all conflicts of interest which might incline an investment adviser—consciously or unconsciously—to render advice which was not disinterested."[7]

There are two duties encompassed in an investment adviser's fiduciary obligation: a duty of care and a duty of loyalty. The duty of care requires the adviser "to provide investment advice in the best interest of its client, based on the client's objectives."[8] The duty of loyalty attaches to the way the adviser does business:

> [An] investment adviser must eliminate or make full and fair disclosure of all conflicts of interest which might incline an investment

---

5. See Commission Interpretation Regarding Standard of Conduct for Investment Advisers, Advisers Act Release No. 5248 (June 5, 2019) ("Fiduciary Interpretation") at footnotes 53–72 and pp. 21–29 for a discussion of how investment advisers satisfy their fiduciary duty when conflicts of interest are present. https://www.sec.gov/rules/interp/2019/ia-5248.pdf.

6. SEC v. Capital Gains Rsch. Bureau, Inc., 375 U.S. 180, 194 (1963).

7. Commission Interpretation Regarding Standard of Conduct for Investment Advisers, U.S. Sec. & Exch. Comm'n, 17 C.F.R. § 276 (2019) 6, https://www.sec.gov/rules/interp/2019/ia-5248.pdf. The term "fiduciary" does not appear in the Advisers Act.

8. *Id.* at 8.

adviser . . . to render advice which is not disinterested such that a client can provide informed consent to the conflict.[9]

Combining the two duties, the SEC noted that in this way, the investment adviser is acting in the client's best interest:

> This combination of care and loyalty obligations has been characterized as requiring the investment adviser to act in the "best interest" of its client at all times. In our view, an investment adviser's obligation to act in the best interest of its client is an overarching principle that encompasses both the duty of care and the duty of loyalty.[10]

Further, the SEC made the point that the fiduciary standard applies to the *entire relationship* with the client.

> The adviser's fiduciary duty is principles-based and *applies to the entire relationship between the adviser and its client*. The fiduciary duty follows the contours of the relationship between the adviser and its client, and the adviser and its client may shape that relationship by agreement, provided that there is full and fair disclosure and informed consent.[11]

When retaining an investment adviser to act on your behalf, the expectation is that the adviser will "adopt the principal's [the client's] goals, objectives, or ends."[12]

Note: The fiduciary standard applies to the entire relationship as defined by the contract between the adviser and the client. That ongoing responsibility is a major differentiator between brokers and advisers.

---

9. *Id.* (emphasis added).
10. *Id.* (emphasis added).
11. *Id.* at 9 (emphasis added).
12. *Id.* at 7–8.

The Broker-Dealer Standard of Care

In its Best Interest adopting release, the SEC stated that the new best interest standard for broker-dealers is "designed to *improve investor protection* by enhancing the quality of broker-dealer recommendations to retail customers and *reducing the potential harm* to retail customers that may be caused by conflicts of interest."[13]

There are also key differences between Regulation Best Interest and the Advisers Act fiduciary standard that reflect the distinction between the services and relationships typically offered under the two business models. "For example, an investment adviser's fiduciary duty generally includes a duty to provide ongoing advice and monitoring, while Regulation Best Interest imposes no such duty and instead requires that a broker-dealer act in the retail customer's best interest *at the time* a recommendation is made."[14]

With that in mind, let's go through the new rule. Note the italicized words:

> A broker, dealer, or a natural person who is an associated person of a broker or dealer, *when making a recommendation* of any securities transaction or investment strategy involving securities (including account recommendations) to a retail customer, shall act in the *best interest* of the retail customer *at the time the recommendation is made*, without placing the financial or other interest of the broker, dealer, or natural person who is an associated person of a broker or dealer making the recommendation ahead of the interest of the retail customer.[15]

There are four elements of the best interest obligation for broker-dealers: the disclosure obligation, care obligation, conflict of interest obligation, and the compliance obligation.[16] Let's review each one.

---

13. Regulation Best Interest: The Broker-Dealer Standard of Conduct, *supra* note 2, at 16 (emphasis added).

14. *Id.* at 17–18.

15. *Id.* at 765 (emphasis added).

16. *See also* SEC Standards of Conduct Rulemaking, https://higherlogicdownload .s3.amazonaws.com/INVESTMENTADVISER/aa03843e-7981-46b2-aa49-c572f2d db7e8/UploadedImages/resources/IAA-Staff-Analysis-Standards-of-Conduct-Rule

Disclosure Obligation

The Best Interest Rule requires written full and fair disclosure of:

(A) All material facts relating to the scope and terms of the relationship with the retail customer, including:
(1) That the broker, dealer, or such natural person is acting as a broker, dealer, or an associated person of a broker or dealer with respect to the recommendation;
(2) The material fees and costs that apply to the retail customer's transactions, holdings, and accounts; and
(3) The type and scope of services provided to the retail customer, including any material limitations on the securities or investment strategies involving securities that may be recommended to the retail customer; and
(B) All material facts relating to conflicts of interest that are associated with the recommendation.[17]

The regulations do not prescribe a specific form for this disclosure. Some firms call their disclosure a "Best Interest Disclosure"; others do not give the disclosure a name. Some have multiple disclosures that are broken up by topics to differentiate different service offerings.

Note: What is important is the breadth of the disclosure obligation, from fees and costs to types and limitations of services, and importantly, from a skeptic's perspective, "all material conflicts of interest . . . associated with the recommendation."

To give you an example of what to expect from a well-crafted best interest disclosure, the following is an excerpt describing the brokerage services of a major dual registrant. Make a note of what the firm says

---

making2.pdf. "When making a recommendation, a broker-dealer must act in the retail customer's best interest and cannot place its own interests ahead of the customer's interests" [hereinafter "General Obligation"]. Regulation Best Interest: The Broker-Dealer Standard of Conduct, *supra* note 2, at 13.

17. Regulation Best Interest: The Broker-Dealer Standard of Conduct, *supra* note 2, at 766 (Emphasis added).

about your responsibility as a client (you are responsible for independently ensuring that the investments are appropriate for you). Also make a note of the fact that the firm has no duty to monitor your investments.

Our responsibilities to you. When you have a brokerage account with us, we have the following responsibilities:

- No monitoring: We have no duty to provide ongoing recommendations or monitor your investments. We are not obligated to provide recommendations to you, or to update recommendations made previously, and not doing so should not be viewed as a recommendation to hold an investment.
- Your responsibility: You are responsible for independently ensuring that the investments in your accounts remain appropriate given your investment objective, risk tolerance, financial circumstances and investment needs.
- Transaction-based compensation: We receive transaction-based compensation for trades you decide to enter into, which includes commissions, administrative fees and compensation from third parties that are disclosed to you.
- No separate fee for advice: Unlike how we charge for investment advisory services, we do not charge or receive a separate fee for our advice or recommendations and our recommendations are provided solely incidental to our brokerage services.[18]

This sample disclosure could not be more clear in its description of services and compensation. I'm sure you will agree that it is essential for you to read disclosures of this type so that you know what to expect, in this case, as a client of a dual registrant acting in its brokerage capacity.

Note: Of the four best interest obligations, the disclosure obligation is most helpful to investors in understanding the scope of the potential engagement.

---

18. Your Relationship with UBS 10, UBS, Sept. 2021, https://www.ubs.com/content/dam/assets/wma/us/shared/documents/relationship-with-ubs.pdf.

Care Obligation

The care obligation focuses on the recommendation and requires the firm and its representative to exercise "reasonable diligence, care, and skill" to:

(A) Understand the potential risks, rewards, and costs associated with the recommendation, and have a reasonable basis to believe that the recommendation *could be in the best interest of at least some retail customers*;

(B) Have a reasonable basis to believe that the recommendation is in the best interest of a particular retail customer based on that retail customer's investment profile and the potential risks, rewards, and costs associated with the recommendation and does not place the financial or other interest of the broker, dealer, or such natural person ahead of the interest of the retail customer;

(C) Have a reasonable basis to believe that a series of recommended transactions, even if in the retail customer's best interest when viewed in isolation, is not excessive and is in the retail customer's best interest when taken together in light of the retail customer's investment profile and does not place the financial or other interest of the broker, dealer, or such natural person making the series of recommendations ahead of the interest of the retail customer.[19]

Satisfying the care obligation needs to rest on an "objective evaluation turning on the facts and circumstances of the particular recommendation and the particular retail customer."[20]

Conflicts of Interest Obligation

Under the conflicts of interest obligation, the broker must establish, maintain, and enforce written policies and procedures reasonably designed to:

19. Regulation Best Interest: The Broker-Dealer Standard of Conduct, *supra* note 2, at 766–67 (emphasis added).
20. *Id.* at 38.

(A) *Identify and at a minimum disclose*, in accordance with paragraph (a)(2)(i) of this section, *or eliminate*, all conflicts of interest associated with such recommendations;

(B) *Identify and mitigate* any conflicts of interest associated with such recommendations that *create an incentive* for a natural person who is an associated person of a broker or dealer to place the interest of the broker, dealer, or such natural person ahead of the interest of the retail customer;

(C)(1) *Identify and disclose* any material limitations placed on the securities or investment strategies involving securities that may be recommended to a retail customer and any conflicts of interest associated with such limitations, in accordance with subparagraph (a)(2)(i), and

(C)(2) *Prevent* such limitations and associated conflicts of interest from causing the broker, dealer, or a natural person who is an associated person of the broker or dealer to make recommendations that place the interest of the broker, dealer, or such natural person ahead of the interest of the retail customer; and

(D) *Identify and eliminate any sales contests, sales quotas, bonuses, and non-cash compensation that are based on the sales of specific securities or specific types of securities within a limited period of time.*[21]

What is conflict? The definition is: "an interest that might incline a broker, dealer, or a natural person who is an associated person of a broker or dealer—*consciously or unconsciously*—to make a recommendation that is not disinterested."[22] Sales contests and compensation based on sales goals are enumerated in the rule. I'll give you examples of other types of conflicts in the next chapter.

---

21. *Id.* at 768 (emphasis added).
22. *Id.* at 36 (emphasis added).

Note: What is a conflict of interest? In laymen's terms, anything that gets in the way of unbiased recommendations, such as a financial incentive that benefits the firm or the representative. The issue for investors is whether they can spot a conflict and determine what to do about it, the subject of the next chapter.

Compliance Obligation

The compliance obligation requires the brokerage firm to establish, maintain, and enforce "written policies and procedures reasonably designed to achieve compliance with Regulation Best Interest."[23]

Note: The compliance obligation is a big "ask" of brokerage firms. We'll see how effective policies and procedures will be over the years as the Best Interest standard of care is implemented and has a chance to develop.

Key Takeaways

This is pretty straightforward: there are differences between investment advisers and brokers even though they might describe their services in a similar fashion. That is, both will be happy to help you with your retirement investments (as will dual registrants, which we will discuss in the next chapter). It is up to you to learn about the differences and determine the services you want.

Consider the following:

- Regulation of brokers is different from regulation of registered investment advisers, *because their service offerings differ.*
- As to legal standards of care, the higher standard (fiduciary) applies to investment advisers. They must subordinate their own interests in the event of a conflict. Importantly, their duty is ongoing, not transactional.

23. *Id.* at 16.

- A transactional service model (broker-dealers) differs from an ongoing management service model (investment advisers). The service model focuses on the transaction, as opposed to an ongoing relationship. The legal standard of care looks to the point of sale (the buy or sell transaction), with no ongoing duty to render advice.
- The SEC considered but declined to "craft a new uniform standard that would apply equally and without differentiation to both broker-dealers and investment advisers."[24]

Next, we'll review conflicts of interest that you can expect to experience as a client of a financial firm, which will give you some insights on what you are willing to accept.

---

24. *Id.* at 20.

Chapter 11
Expect to Experience Conflicts of Interest, but Choose Not To

---

Note: Conflicts of interest are not that easy for individuals to spot. The purpose of this chapter is to share some examples from publicly available disclosures. The source of this information is SEC filings and SEC actions. Some settlements are negotiated, with firms neither admitting nor denying allegations or findings.

In the chapter, you will see examples of conflicted situations, along with boxed "Disclosure Notes" that provide a summary of the firm's disclosures. Firms are not identified by name.

No matter the type of firm you choose to engage in retirement, you will encounter business practices that pose conflicts. Conflicts are inevitable in every type of firm, whether a stand-alone adviser, stand-alone broker, or dual registrant. However, they are not uniformly present in all environments, giving you the option to side-step them (something consumers may not realize they can do). Business practices vary from firm to firm, even when comparing dual registrants to other dual registrants or investment advisers to other investment advisers. Distinctions between a dual registrant and a stand-alone adviser are more easily identified, due to differences in business models.

Note: There are firms that are structured to *avoid* common conflicts tied to product sales. That means you can choose to avoid environments where financial incentives can interfere with unbiased advice, a benefit during retirement, when expertise and trust are paramount to promote a safe, secure, and happy retirement.

Because you can make choices only if you are aware, I've done some digging through enforcement and regulatory actions and disclosure documents, which I will share with you in this chapter. *The discussion starts with dual registrants to give you the benefit of both types of disclosure documents you'll want to be familiar with, "Form ADV"*[1] *for investment advisers and a "Detailed Report"*[2] *for broker-dealers.* Dual registrants must file both reports with the SEC. You will be able to access reports on the firm level and the individual representative level.[3]

Now, let's discuss the role of the firm and the representative in the "dually hatted" environment of a dual registrant. We'll look at managed accounts, mutual funds, variable annuities, 529 plans, unit investment trusts, and bond purchases. Then, we'll look at stand-alone investment advisers. Finally, we'll address a question that I'm anticipating will cross your mind: *Is there such a thing as a conflict-free firm (or representative)?*

Note: In Chapter 15, we'll discuss how to put conflicts of interest into context for yourself when comparing firms.

Dual Registrant Representatives Wear Two Hats

A critical element to understand when engaging with a dual registrant is the dually hatted nature of the representative's role. The dually-registered representative is able to act in two capacities: either as a representative of an investment adviser (fiduciary duty) or a representative of a broker-dealer (best interest).[4] That's a complication for a client, when it comes down to assessing potential conflicts of interest. In a way, you might want to think of a dually hatted representative as a free agent—free to move from one role to another.

---

1. https://adviserinfo.sec.gov/.

2. https://brokercheck.finra.org/.

3. Also, you can review an investment adviser's relationship with broker-dealers in Form ADV Part 2A or Part 2A Appendix 1 also called "Part 2 Brochures" (see Items 4, 5E, 8, 10, 11, 12, and 14 in Form ADV Part 2A and Items 4, 6, and 9 of Part 2A Appendix 1) and in Form ADV Part 1A (see Items 5, 6, 7, 8), both of which you can find on the SEC website at https://adviserinfo.sec.gov/.

4. Not all brokers are also registered as investment adviser representatives. You'll have to ask.

This is how the SEC expressed the dynamic for a person who works for a dual registrant. Notice that the standard that applies depends on the capacity in which the representative is acting:

Where a financial professional who is dually registered (i.e., an associated person of a broker-dealer and a supervised person of an investment adviser (regardless of whether the professional works for a dual-registrant, affiliated firm, or unaffiliated firm)) is making an account recommendation to a retail customer, *whether Regulation Best Interest or the Advisers Act will apply will depend on the capacity in which the financial professional making the recommendation is acting.*[5]

The SEC is pointing out an important foundational concept that clients of a dually registered firm must understand. Your dually-registered representative can act in the capacity of:

1. a supervised person of an investment adviser, or
2. a supervised person of a broker-dealer ("registered representative").

If your representative works for a dual registrant and is registered as an investment adviser representative and a registered representative, he or she is "dually hatted."

A dually hatted individual can act in either capacity. If acting in the investment advisory capacity, the Advisers Act applies. When acting in a brokerage capacity, the 1934 Act applies and so does the new Regulation Best Interest.

What does this mean to you if your representative is dually hatted? In practical terms, it makes life a little more complicated. The representative can switch hats, and it is up to you to identify when that happens. That's extra effort on your behalf at a time when you might prefer a more regimented environment where hat switching does not occur (stand-alone investment advisers with no third-party arrangements with broker-dealers).

---

5. Regulation Best Interest: The Broker-Dealer Standard of Conduct, U.S. Sec. & Exch. Comm'n, 17 C.F.R. § 240 (2019) 99, https://www.sec.gov/rules/final/2019/34 -86031.pdf. Effective Sept. 10, 2019 (emphasis added).

To give you an idea of what one might expect as a client of a dually hatted representative when things go awry, read the following example of hat switching.

Example of "Hat Switching"

This is an example of an SEC enforcement[6] action against a dual registrant that will help you understand some of the nuances you can run into with a dually hatted representative.

The SEC concluded that the firm's dually hatted representatives were unable to keep the duties demanded of the roles of adviser and broker separate.

> [The firm] employs [representatives] who are both registered as broker-dealer representatives and licensed as investment adviser representatives of [the firm]. During the Relevant Period, the [representatives] purportedly engaged in "hat switching" between these dual roles during the course of interacting with [retirement plan] participants and depending on the activity.[7]

Quoting the SEC, the firm's representatives themselves were "frequently confused about their various roles, including whether they were acting as an investment adviser representative or registered representative when recommending rollovers into [the managed account[8] program]."[9]

The firm's "disclosures and misleading statements downplayed and obscured financial incentives that created conflicts between it and its [representatives] on one hand and its clients on the other," reported the SEC's Enforcement Division.[10]

---

6. The SEC Enforcement Division's mission is "to protect investors and the markets by investigating potential violations of the federal securities laws and litigating the SEC's enforcement actions." U.S. Sec. & Exch. Comm'n Division of Enforcement, *Enforcement Manual*, https://www.sec.gov/divisions/enforce/enforcementmanual.pdf.

7. Firm A: U.S. Sec. & Exch. Comm'n Cease-and-Desist Order, 2021. To find Cease and Desist Orders, search at sec.gov.

8. A managed account is a brokerage account that is composed of individual securities overseen by an investment adviser.

9. Firm A: U.S. Sec. & Exch. Comm'n Cease-and-Desist Order, 2021.

10. Firm A: U.S. Sec. & Exch. Comm'n Press Release, 2021.

The firm's representatives were trained to tell clients "that they offered 'objective' and 'non-commissioned' advice, 'put the client first,' and acted in the client's best interest while holding themselves out as fiduciaries."[11]

SEC Enforcement found this to be misleading "because [the firm's] financial incentives for [representatives] rendered their advice non-objective and [the firm] did not ensure that [its representatives'] recommendations were, in fact, in the best interest of its clients."[12]

Further, the firm "simultaneously applied continual pressure to compel [its representatives] to prioritize the rollover of [retirement] assets into [the managed accounts] over lower cost alternatives."[13]

The firm agreed to a censure and payment of $97 million, which included a civil penalty of $9 million. The firm also agreed to notify clients that were affected, review disclosures relating to managed accounts, improve training of its representatives, and to cease and desist from committing future violations of the Advisers Act. One positive outcome was the firm's elimination of differential compensation for managed accounts and an adoption of fiduciary standards for managed accounts recommendations.

Disclosure Note: The firm reported this disciplinary matter as number one of five in its 44-page "Detailed Report" on Broker-Check. The report contained 18 pages of Disclosure Events (five regulatory events and four arbitrations).[14] The firm's ADV is 81 pages long. Item 11 Disclosure Information starts on page 52; Disclosure Reporting is found on pages 56 to 79.[15] Look for ADVs on the SEC's website at https://adviserinfo.sec.gov/. Look for Broker-Check on FINRA's website at https://brokercheck.finra.org/.

---

11. *Id.*
12. *Id.*
13. *Id.*
14. Firm A: BrokerCheck Detailed Report © 2022 FINRA. All rights reserved. FINRA is a registered trademark of the Financial Industry Regulatory Authority, Inc. Reprinted with permission from FINRA. Detailed Report accessed on February 23, 2022.
15. Firm A: ADV 2022. ADV accessed February 23, 2022.

What led to these events? As reported in the Enforcement Action, 20 years earlier, the firm noted it was losing business to other firms when a retirement plan participant became eligible to rollover assets to other firms (retirement, in service withdrawals, etc.) A few years later, the firm began offering the managed account service and incented its representatives to recommend managed accounts through a bonus program. For example, top performers (meaning top salesmen), could earn a bonus of two times to nearly seven times their base salary.

The firm's "sales strategy, incentive compensation plan and negative pressures" on its representatives worked. The firm opened over 18,000 new managed accounts and revenues grew exponentially (from $2.6 million to $54 million from 1/1/2013 to 3/30/2018).[16]

Note: This Enforcement Action underlines the importance of not only understanding potential conflicts of interest, but also illustrates how sales pressures and sales incentives can influence a recommendation. It also presents a question to consider: Should a discerning investor try to avoid potentially conflicted environments? How would investors recognize such environments? The CRS is the starting point (Chapter 12).

Example of a Variable Annuity Sales Conflict

If you have been offered or own a variable annuity, you may be familiar with switching violations. For example, FINRA ordered a dual registrant to pay a fine of $675,000 and to make restitution of $1.4 million to 100 customers for failing to supervise representatives who made unsuitable recommendations to their customers to switch from one product to another.

As an example, a representative recommended that a customer liquidate a variable annuity in favor of a mutual fund. The recommendation resulted in the customer paying a surrender charge of $5,070. The surrender value of $126,681 then was used to purchase mutual funds with upfront sales charges of $5,531. Was that recommendation to the customer's advantage? No. FINRA reported: "The recommended switch

---

16. Firm A: U.S. Sec. & Exch. Comm'n Cease-and-Desist Order, 2021.

resulted in the customer earning less annual income than she would have earned had she not sold the variable annuity."[17]

Disclosure Note: The firm's "Detailed Report" at BrokerCheck reported this disciplinary matter as number six of 170 Regulatory Events. The Detailed Report consists of 501 pages, 474 of which are Disclosure Events (170 Regulatory Events, two Civil Events, and 298 Arbitrations).[18] The ADV is 798 pages long. Item 11 Disclosure Information starts on page 43; Disclosure Reporting begins on page 47 and ends on page 796.[19]

In this case, the firm did not follow its own supervisory procedures to send "switch letters" to customers confirming that they understood the ramifications of the recommendation.

Example of a 529 Plan Conflict

You may be familiar with 529 education savings plans. Like mutual funds they also may have share class differences. In this case, a dual registrant paid restitution of about $1 million to compensate purchasers of a Class C 529 plan recommended by the firm's representatives. Class C shares can be more expensive (and pay the broker more) over longer periods of time, such as can be expected when a 529 is purchased for a young child for college funding.

> Broker-sold 529 plans often use load-waived shares of mutual funds as components of their plan portfolios, and include sales charges and/or asset-based distribution fees at the 529 plan portfolio level. 529 plan Class A units are offered pursuant to a front-end sales load and an annualized asset-based fee. 529 plan Class C units typically are not subject to a front-end load, but generally include higher annualized asset-based fees than Class A units. As

---

17. Firm B: Financial Industry Regulatory Authority Press Release. © 2020 FINRA. All rights reserved. FINRA is a registered trademark of the Financial Industry Regulatory Authority, Inc. Reprinted with permission.

18. Firm B: BrokerCheck Detailed Report. © 2022 FINRA. All rights reserved. FINRA is a registered trademark of the Financial Industry Regulatory Authority, Inc. Reprinted with permission from FINRA. Detailed Report accessed on February 23, 2022.

19. Firm B: ADV, 2022. ADV accessed on February 23, 2022.

a result, Class A units may often be less expensive over extended holding periods than Class C units, despite being subject to an initial front-end sales load.[20]

This dual registrant's Best Interest Disclosure pointed out that compensation for 529 plans varied based on the 529 class that the customer purchases.[21]

Disclosure Note: This firm's "Detailed Report" disclosed this regulatory action as disclosure number 25 of 587 disclosures. The 1,690-page long report contained 1,653 pages of Disclosure Events, including 587 Regulatory Events, four Civil Events and 873 Arbitrations.[22] The ADV is 617 pages long. Item 11 Disclosure Information starts at page 78; Disclosure Reporting begins on page 83 and ends on page 615.[23]

Another dual registrant was censured, fined, and paid restitution of about $1.7 million to 2,293 customers in connection with 529 plans.[24] In that case, FINRA pointed out that:

A customer who initially invested $10,000 in Class C shares and held those shares for eighteen years would pay approximately $1,300 more in fees and expenses than if the customer had invested the same amount in Class A shares. Moreover, the customer's 529 plan account for this period would be worth approximately $1,500 less than an account that instead was invested in Class A shares.[25]

---

20. Firm C: Financial Industry Regulatory Authority Letter of Acceptance, Waiver and Consent. © 2019 FINRA. All rights reserved. FINRA is a registered trademark of the Financial Industry Regulatory Authority, Inc. Reprinted with permission.

21. Firm C: Best Interest Disclosure Statement, 2021.

22. Firm C: BrokerCheck Detailed Report. © 2022 FINRA. All rights reserved. FINRA is a registered trademark of the Financial Industry Regulatory Authority, Inc. Reprinted with permission from FINRA. Detailed Report accessed on February 23, 2022.

23. Firm C: ADV, 2022. ADV accessed on February 23, 2022.

24. Firm D: Financial Industry Regulatory Authority Letter of Acceptance, Waiver and Consent. © 2020 FINRA. All rights reserved. FINRA is a registered trademark of the Financial Industry Regulatory Authority, Inc. Reprinted with permission.

25. *Id.*

As a result of gaps in the firm's supervisory system, over $180 million of 529 plan class C shares were "inconsistent with the share class suggested by the firm's grids. These purchases should have been, but were not, subject to further supervisory review under the firm's procedures."[26]

This dual registrant's disclosures pointed out that fees for 529 plans varied based on the 529 class that the customer purchases.[27]

Disclosure Note: This firm's "Detailed Report" listed this regulatory action as disclosure number two of 56. The 260-page report contained 215 pages of Disclosure Events, including 101 Arbitrations, adding up to 157 total disclosures.[28] The ADV is 382 pages long. Item 11 Disclosure Information starts with page 146; Disclosure Reporting is on pages 151–379.[29]

Example of a Mutual Fund Share Class Conflict

It's hard to imagine a potential conflict of interest when you purchase mutual funds. Not all mutual fund investors[30] are aware that a single mutual fund may have a number of different share classes that are priced differently. Some share classes offer sales charge waivers. Some share classes pay no incentives to firms or representatives and, as a result, are less costly to the investor, while avoiding conflicts caused by financial incentives.[31]

---

26. *Id.*

27. Firm D: Understanding 529 Education Savings Plans and Compensation, 2022.

28. Firm D: BrokerCheck Detailed Report. © 2022 FINRA. All rights reserved. FINRA is a registered trademark of the Financial Industry Regulatory Authority, Inc. Reprinted with permission. Detailed Report accessed on February 23, 2022.

29. Firm D: ADV, 2022. ADV accessed on February 23, 2022.

30. Over one hundred million investors own mutual funds, according to the Investment Company Institute. *2021 Investment Company Fact Book*, https://www.icifactbook.org/21_fb_ch3.html.

31. For example, Investment Company of America has 21 share classes (each with a unique symbol). Pricing varies based on whether the fund is offered through a 529 plan, retirement plan, or other type of account (for example, an individual account, a joint account, or a transfer on death account). The prospectus points out up front sales charges, deferred sales charges, charges on reinvested dividends, and waivers. https://www.capitalgroup.com/us/pdf/shareholder/mfgeipx-004_icap.pdf.

In noncommissioned environments, a firm can offer a low-cost institutional share class with no sales charges or ongoing fees (12b-1 fees).[32] Generally, the institutional share class pays no direct or indirect payments to the firm or to a representative.

Note: Mutual fund share class conflicts of interest could arise with a dual registrant or a stand-alone broker-dealer. What about a stand-alone investment adviser? Generally, the answer is no. The exceptions are (1) the stand-alone adviser has an affiliated broker-dealer; or (2) a representative of the adviser is registered with an affiliated or unaffiliated broker-dealer. You can find this information in the firm's Form ADV and Form ADV Part 2A (also called the "Brochure"), both of which are available on the SEC's website.[33]

As a client, you want to know whether the representative is incentivized to recommend a share class that pays him or her more than another choice.

Share classes are disclosed in prospectuses,[34] along with upfront sales charges, deferred sales charges, charges on reinvested dividends, sales charge reductions and waivers, redemption fees or exchange fees that are paid directly from your investment in the fund. Other fees are operating expenses, such as management fees, distribution and service fees ("12b-1 fees"), and other expenses. The fund's trading costs (for buying and selling the fund's investments) are imbedded in the price of fund shares.[35] Appendix B provides an example of share class prospectus disclosure.

---

32. See, for example, Investment Company of America F-3 shares in prospectus at https://www.capitalgroup.com/us/pdf/shareholder/mfgeipx-004_icap.pdf.

33. You can look up broker-dealer relationships in Form ADV Part 2A also called "Part 2 Brochure" (see items 5 and 10) and in Form ADV (see Items 5E, 6, 7, 8), both of which you can find on the SEC website at https://adviserinfo.sec.gov/.

34. Mutual funds are regulated under the Investment Company Act of 1940; prospectus disclosure is mandated for mutual funds under the same requirements of the Securities Act of 1933 that apply generally to issuers of securities issuers.

35. You can search for mutual fund prospectuses on the SEC's website at https://www.sec.gov/edgar/searchedgar/prospectus.htm. For an example, see the prospectus for Vanguard Wellington Fund at https://advisors.vanguard.com/pub/Pdf/p021.pdf. Turnover is relevant in assessing the effect of trading costs on returns.

Note: Some firms permit representatives to offer different share classes of mutual funds; others do not. This is a data point to consider when you are thinking about how to formulate your personal selection criteria, the subject of Chapter 15.

As an example, FINRA found that a major dual registrant "disadvantaged tens of thousands of small business retirement plan customers that were eligible to purchase Class A shares in certain mutual funds without a sales charge but were instead sold mutual funds with a front-end sales charge or Class B or C shares with back-end sales charges and higher ongoing fees and expenses."[36] Over a period of five years, the matter affected about 28,000 small business 401(k) and other retirement plan accounts, whose participants qualified for, but did not receive the benefit of, the available sales charge waiver.

According to FINRA's Department of Enforcement, the dual registrant had "learned of this problem in 2006 but elected not to notify its sales force and its customers that certain retirement plans could be eligible for sales charge waivers, and did not report its findings to FINRA until November 2011."[37]

Disclosure Note: The firm reported this disciplinary matter as number 125 of 587. The 1,690-page "Detailed Report" on BrokerCheck contained 1,652 pages of Disclosure Events (including four Civil Events, and 873 Arbitrations) for a total of 1,464 total disclosures.[38] The ADV is 617 pages long. Item 11 Disclosure Information starts at page 76; Disclosure Reporting begins on page 83 and ends on page 615.[39]

---

36. Firm C: Financial Industry Regulatory Authority Letter of Acceptance, Waiver and Consent. © 2014 FINRA. All rights reserved. FINRA is a registered trademark of the Financial Industry Regulatory Authority, Inc. Reprinted with permission from FINRA.

37. *Id.*

38. Firm C: BrokerCheck Detailed Report. © 2022 FINRA. All rights reserved. FINRA is a registered trademark of the Financial Industry Regulatory Authority, Inc. Reprinted with permission from FINRA. Detailed Report accessed on February 23, 2022.

39. Firm C: ADV, 2022. ADV accessed on February 23, 2022.

In another mutual fund situation, FINRA censured and fined a dual registrant that failed to provide 35,000 customers with sales charge waivers that they were entitled to.[40] The firm paid customers restitution of $15 million ($13 million due to customers being overcharged, plus interest).

Disclosure Note: The firm reported this disciplinary matter in its "Detailed Report" on BrokerCheck (number 30 of 170). The "Detailed Report" of 501 pages contained 474 pages of Disclosure Events, including 170 Regulatory Events, two Civil Events, and 298 Arbitrations.[41] The ADV is 798 pages long. Item 11 Disclosure Information starts on page 43; Disclosure Reporting begins on page 47 and ends on page 796.[42]

Example of a Unit Investment Trust Conflict

FINRA ordered another dual registrant to pay more than $8.4 million in restitution to more than 3,000 customers, plus a fine of $3.25 million for failure to supervise brokers who recommended early unit investment trust (UIT) rollovers.[43]

When a representative recommends a sale of a UIT before the maturity date and then "rolls over" those funds into a new UIT, that "causes the customer to incur increased sales charges over time, raising suitability concerns," reported FINRA.[44]

---

40. Firm B: Financial Industry Regulatory Authority Letter of Acceptance, Waiver and Consent. © 2015 FINRA. All rights reserved. FINRA is a registered trademark of the Financial Industry Regulatory Authority, Inc. Reprinted with permission.

41. Firm B: BrokerCheck Detailed Report. © 2022 FINRA. All rights reserved. FINRA is a registered trademark of the Financial Industry Regulatory Authority, Inc. Reprinted with permission from FINRA. Detailed Report accessed on February 23, 2022.

42. Firm B: ADV, 2022. ADV accessed on February 23, 2022.

43. Firm C: Financial Industry Regulatory Authority Press Release. © 2021 FINRA. All rights reserved. FINRA is a registered trademark of the Financial Industry Regulatory Authority, Inc. Reprinted with permission from FINRA.

44. *Id.*

Disclosure Note: The firm reported this disciplinary matter as number seven of 587. It was also reported by FINRA on June 25, 2021.[45] The 1,690-page "Detailed Report" on BrokerCheck contained 1,652 pages of Disclosure Events (including four Civil Events, and 873 Arbitrations) for a total of 1,464 total disclosures. The ADV is 617 pages long. Item 11 Disclosure Information starts at page 78; Disclosure Reporting begins on page 83 and ends on page 615.[46]

Example of Bond Purchases and Sales

The following illustration shows how compensation tied to trading activities can incentivize a representative.

In this situation, a representative's activity in bonds for ten of his customers cost them losses of about $775,000 plus interest. The representative's firm, a major dual registrant, was censured, fined $175,000, and required to pay restitution of about $900,000.

This was one customer's experience:

[O]n or around September 18, 2013, [the representative] recommended that a customer (the "Customer") purchase $65,000 in corporate bonds issued by an insurance company. Fewer than two months later, on or about November 11, 2013, [the representative] recommended that the Customer sell the bonds, at a loss, and use the proceeds to purchase $63,800 in bonds issued by a bank. Approximately four months later, [the representative] recommended that the Customer sell those bonds, also at a loss, and use the proceeds to purchase $61,200 in bonds issued by a telecommunications company. [The representative] recommended that the Customer sell a portion of those bonds on or about June 9, 2014, at a loss and after holding them for fewer than three months.

---

45. Firm C: BrokerCheck Detailed Report. © 2022 FINRA. All rights reserved. FINRA is a registered trademark of the Financial Industry Regulatory Authority, Inc. Reprinted with permission from FINRA. Detailed Report accessed on February 23, 2022.

46. Firm C: ADV, 2022. ADV accessed on February 23, 2022.

Collectively, those recommended securities transactions required the Customer to pay more than $5,500 in sales charges and resulted in more than $2,500 in net losses, which were inclusive of sales charges paid by the Customer, minus any interest payments received by the Customer.[47]

When a representative recommends buying and then selling bonds within a short period of time, the customer needs to be on high alert. High turnover does not fit the risk/reward profile of a typical retirement account.

Disclosure Note: On BrokerCheck, the firm's "Detailed Report" listed this regulatory action as disclosure number three of 56. The report, 260 pages long, contained 214 pages of Disclosure Events, including 56 Regulatory Events and 101 Arbitrations.[48] The ADV is 382 pages long. Item 11 Disclosure Information starts with page 146; Disclosure Reporting is on pages 151 to 379.[49]

Investment Adviser Conflicts

Third Party Payments

Just as with dual registrants, investment adviser conflicts center around financial incentives. You'll want to understand arrangements in which advisers get paid by *someone other than you*, the client. Such arrangements can potentially influence the adviser to make recommendations that benefit the firm or representative instead of the client.

The SEC offered this perspective:

An adviser that receives, directly or indirectly, compensation in connection with the investments it recommends has a financial

---

47. Firm D: Financial Industry Regulatory Authority Letter of Acceptance, Waiver and Consent. © 2020 FINRA. All rights reserved. FINRA is a registered trademark of the Financial Industry Regulatory Authority, Inc. Reprinted with permission.

48. Firm D: BrokerCheck Detailed Report. © 2022 FINRA. All rights reserved. FINRA is a registered trademark of the Financial Industry Regulatory Authority, Inc. Reprinted with permission from FINRA. Detailed Report accessed February 23, 2022.

49. Firm D: ADV, 2022. ADV accessed February 23, 2022.

incentive to make recommendations that result in the receipt of that compensation. Depending on the nature of the compensation, this financial incentive would give rise to conflicts relating to, for example, the types of investments, the fund families, the particular funds and the share classes of individual funds that the adviser recommends, as well as the extent of trading it recommends. For instance, when an adviser receives, directly or indirectly, 12b-1 fees in connection with mutual fund recommendations, it has a financial incentive to recommend that a client invest in a share class that pays 12b-1 fees. The resulting conflict of interest is especially pronounced when share classes of the same funds that do not bear these fees are available to the client.[50]

To find these additional financial incentives, consider if there is a third party involved, namely a broker-dealer, an insurance company that offers retirement income products, or an issuer or product sponsor.

When we refer to advisers receiving 12b-1 fees or other compensation "directly or indirectly," we are including (a) advisers that are also registered broker-dealers and receive 12b-1 fees or other compensation, (b) advisers whose affiliated broker-dealers receive 12b-1 fees or other compensation or (c) advisers whose supervised or associated persons receive 12b-1 fees or other compensation as registered representatives of *affiliated or unaffiliated broker-dealers.*[51]

This leads to whether conflicts can be avoided through the choice of a fiduciary investment adviser.

Fiduciary Status Is Not Enough

Even though investment advisers are fiduciaries by law, that does not mean they are conflict-free.

---

50. *Frequently Asked Questions Regarding Disclosure of Certain Financial Conflicts Related to Investment Adviser Compensation*, U.S. Sec. & Exch. Comm'n (last modified Oct. 18, 2019), https://www.sec.gov/investment/faq-disclosure-conflicts-invest ment-adviser-compensation.

51. *Id.* (emphasis added).

Regarding conflicts, the SEC noted:

> The investment adviser-client relationship also has inherent con-
> flicts of interest, including those resulting from an asset-based
> compensation structure that may provide an incentive for an
> investment adviser to encourage its client to invest more money
> through an adviser in order increase its AUM [assets under man-
> agement] at the expense of the client.[52]

Direct Payments from the Client

In an environment in which the adviser charges an asset-based fee, which
is typical in the industry, the incentive is to encourage a client to invest
more. In and of itself, that's not a conflict unless the advice is "at the
expense of the client."[53] An example might be increasing AUM by recommending a 401(k) rollover to an IRA under the firm's management if the
rollover negatively impacts the client.[54]

For more information on researching investment advisers, see Appendix D on Form ADV and Appendix E on ADV disclosure information.

Is There Such a Thing as a Conflict-Free Firm or Representative?

You may be wondering: Is there such as thing as a conflict-free firm? The
short answer is that you can get pretty close, but no firm is *completely*
free of all potential conflicts. Having reviewed disclosure documents of
dual registrants and stand-alone advisers, my own observation is this:
Firms range from multiple conflicts to hardly any.

It all comes down to financial incentives and firm culture. The firms
that have fewer financial incentives win that race. If you ask me what

---

52. Regulation Best Interest: The Broker-Dealer Standard of Conduct, *supra* note 5,
at 7, footnote 6.

53. *Id.*

54. The Department of Labor (DOL) Fiduciary Rules issued on April 13, 2021, provide guidance on the prohibited transaction exemption pertaining to fiduciary investment advice for retirement investors, employee benefit plans and investment advice
providers. See DOL, New Fiduciary Advice Exemption: PTE 2020-02 Improving Investment Advice for Workers & Retirees Frequently Asked Questions at https://www.dol
.gov/sites/dolgov/files/ebsa/about-ebsa/our-activities/resource-center/faqs/new-fiduciary
-advice-exemption.pdf.

that type of firm might look like, I can offer my *biased* perspective as an industry insider who runs a stand-alone adviser that is independent of broker-dealer affiliations. Here it is: Because financial incentives and culture foment conflicts, I advise you to focus on *how the firm makes money. Form CRS will help you do that (see Chapter 12).* The cleanest situation is a firm whose revenue is generated exclusively by direct payments from the client (for example, management or consulting fees). That means no other source of revenue (from third parties[55] or other revenue streams[56]) gets in the way of a recommendation; it also means there is no incentive for a transactional advantage to be gained through the types of conflicts that are discussed in this chapter. This observation holds true whether the firm is a mega dual registrant or a small stand-alone investment adviser.[57]

Seeing how incentives can affect a recommendation is key to understanding conflicts of interest that present themselves in different environments. Any firm that incentivizes representatives or itself receives financial incentives for taking one course of action over another can increase the need for vigilance. That is, it puts you in the position of having to be alert to the nature of the recommendation to see if it is indeed in your interest, not the firm's or the representative's.

Due Diligence Efforts Depend on Business Models

Conflicts arise out of business practices, and business practices differ from firm to firm, flowing from the vision of the firm's leadership. Very large dual registrants that have multiple lines of business and thousands or tens of thousands of representatives are far more complex than stand-alone advisers.

---

55. For example, revenue sharing or direct third-party payments.

56. For example, sales of proprietary products manufactured by the firm or an affiliate; principal trading, where the firm buys or sells an investment to or from a client from the firm's own accounts; or benefiting from a trade at the expense of a client. See Chapter 12.

57. For a stand-alone adviser to receive incentives based on transactions, the firm would typically have a broker-dealer relationship. The relationship is either directly through a related party or through a representative who works for the adviser but also is a registered representative of an unaffiliated broker-dealer. You can look up broker-dealer relationships in Form ADV Part 2A, also called "Part 2 Brochures" (see items 5 and 10) and in Form ADV (see Items 5E, 6, 7, 8), both of which you can find on the SEC website at https://adviserinfo.sec.gov/.

The close to 13,000 SEC-registered stand-alone investment advisers[58] are primarily small firms, each having a personality, culture, and value system that embodies the firm's founders. Some have a simple business model with a single focus on the needs of the client; some add complexity when they inject third parties into the mix. More complexity calls for layers of disclosure (both 1934 Act and Advisers Act) and more time and effort for reasoned due diligence.[59] Less complexity makes the due diligence process less taxing. That's simply the nature of the due diligence exercise.

Key Takeaways

You can find conflicts with dual registrants, stand-alone advisers and stand-alone broker-dealers. Conflicts are not uniform across financial firms, nor are they ubiquitous. They vary based on service, whether transaction based as with a broker-dealer or dual registrant, and culture, whether sales and revenue generation are incentivized or not. That's why it's important to understand the firm's business environment in advance of retaining a firm or representative. It's also important to learn the role of the representative. The best way to start the inquiry is Form CRS, the subject of the next chapter.

---

58. Regulation Best Interest: The Broker-Dealer Standard of Conduct, *supra* note 5, at 413.

59. Professor Nicole Boyson (Northeastern U.), *The Worst of Both Worlds? Dual-Registered Investment Advisers* (2019) explores business models, conflicts, fees, and reviews disciplinary data, https://www1.villanova.edu/content/dam/villanova/VSB/under grad/Boyson-The-worst-of-both-worlds-Dual-registered-investment-advisers.pdf.

Chapter 12
Form CRS Is Key

Before the Client (or Customer) Relationship Summary (Form CRS) arrived on the scene in 2020, investors were at a distinct disadvantage when searching for an appropriate financial firm to retain—there was no efficient way to compare firms, their services, their conflicts of interest, and their disciplinary histories. In fact, it would not surprise me if your financial representative found you, instead of you initiating a search, applying selection criteria that you created for your unique situation.

With the CRS, you'll be able to get a sense of the firm you now work with and compare others that you may want to retain for retirement investing. As you read ahead, keep track of what is important to you in a relationship; we'll incorporate your views into a personal rule set in Chapters 14 and 15.

First Things First: The Firm

Given that we now have the CRS, you can easily take initiative.

The order of operations one would follow may be counterintuitive. Your first decision is what type of firm would be best for you based not only on the service needed (as discussed in Parts I and II of this book) but also on the type of client experience you would like to have. The secondary decision is the choice of representative.

Why this order? Remember: not all financial service providers are the same. Different firms provide different services and means of delivering a client experience. Moreover, individual representatives can and do switch firms, so a representative who is a good fit today may be in a different firm and providing different services tomorrow.

The goal of the CRS review is to identify those firms that you will want to eliminate and those that you will want to consider in more depth.

How to Read the CRS

The CRS is a short disclosure document. The acronym stands for Customer (or Client) Relationship Summary.[1] The CRS is mandated for all SEC-regulated financial firms (registered investment advisers, broker-dealers, and dual registrants). Other financial firms, such as insurance agencies, trust companies, and banks, do not have a CRS disclosure obligation.

The best way to review a firm's CRS is to compare it to another firm's CRS. To find the CRS of the firm you now work with, go to your firm's website or BrokerCheck, which is operated by FINRA.[2] (You'll be able to search for both broker-dealers and investment advisers there.) On BrokerCheck, the CRS is referred to as the "Relationship Summary." In the footnote, I've provided a few randomly chosen samples.[3] While "Conversation Starters" are incorporated into the CRS, I'm leaving them for discussion in Chapter 13. These are questions the SEC would like you to ask your representative so that you have a better understanding of the firm.

The SEC prescribes the order and content of the CRS.[4] Let's go through each item one by one. As you read ahead, think about how you would

---

1. Form CRS Relationship Summary: Amendments to Form ADV, U.S. Sec. & Exch. Comm'n, 17 C.F.R. §§ 200, 240, 249, 275, 279 (2019), https://www.sec.gov/rules/final /2019/34-86032.pdf. *See also* the SEC's investor.gov site, https://www.investor.gov/CRS.

2. BrokerCheck is at https://brokercheck.finra.org/. FINRA (the Financial Industry Regulatory Authority) is a not-for-profit, self-regulatory organization (SRO) responsible for regulating its member broker-dealers and their associated persons pursuant to the 1934 Act. © 2022 FINRA. All rights reserved. FINRA is a registered trademark of the Financial Industry Regulatory Authority, Inc. Reprinted with permission from FINRA.

3. Start with https://brokercheck.finra.org/ and search for a familiar name and click on "Relationship Summary." For example, Merrill Lynch (Merrill Lynch, Pierce, Fenner & Smith at https://files.brokercheck.finra.org/crs_7691.pdf); UBS (UBS Financial Services at https://files.brokercheck.finra.org/crs_8174.pdf); Fidelity (Fidelity Brokerage Services at https://files.brokercheck.finra.org/crs_7784.pdf); Vanguard (Vanguard Brokerage Services®—called Vanguard Marketing Corporation at https://files.brokercheck.finra.org/crs _7452.pdf), © 2022 FINRA. All rights reserved. FINRA is a registered trademark of the Financial Industry Regulatory Authority, Inc. Reprinted with permission from FINRA.

4. "Form CRS Appendix A: General Instructions" and "Form CRS Appendix B: Instructions to Form CRS.\" are set out in the adopting release: https://www.sec.gov

create search criteria for the firm you would like to retain, whether that be your current financial firm, or another. We'll return to this subject in Chapters 13 and 14 when we discuss your personal views. Watch for business practices and conflicts of interest for the firm and its representatives.

Item 1. Introduction

The firm must provide an introduction to the firm's type of business, whether a stand-alone broker-dealer, stand-alone investment adviser, or a dual registrant (registered as both a broker-dealer and an investment adviser).[5]

Note: When you compare the CRS of one firm to another's, separate them by how they are regulated. Dual registrants will have a four-page CRS (or two two-page Forms CRS, one for brokerage services and one for advisory services). Stand-alone firm CRSs will be two pagers. You can tell the difference between advisers and brokers by the service description.

Item 2. Relationships and Services

"What investment services and advice can you provide me?"[6]

In its description, the firm must address four specific areas:

1. Whether the firm monitors the investments, including the frequency and any material limitations with respect to monitoring[7]
2. The firm's investment authority (discretionary or not)[8]
3. Whether investment offerings are limited (proprietary products, for example)[9]

/rules/final/2019/34-86032.pdf. See also Form ADV, Part 3: Instructions to Form CRS at https://www.sec.gov/about/forms/formadv-part3.pdf.

5. Form CRS Relationship Summary: Amendments to Form ADV, U.S. Securities and Exchange Commission, 17 C.F.R. § 249.640 (2019) 10, https://www.sec.gov/rules/final/2019/34-86032-appendix-b.pdf. CRS Instructions for Item 1.

6. *Id.* CRS Instructions for Item 2.

7. *Id.* CRS Instructions for Item 2(B)(i).

8. *Id.* CRS Instructions for Item 2(B)(ii).

9. *Id.* at 11. CRS Instructions for Item 2(B)(iii).

4. The firm's account minimums and other requirements (for example, minimums for opening or maintaining an account or a relationship)[10]

Note: When you compare firms, you will see distinctions that can help you determine whether the firm fits your needs. For retirement investing, if you want personal portfolio management (Chapter 1), you'll want to see that the firm provides monitoring services and has discretionary investment authority to manage your portfolio. If the firm offers investment offerings that are limited to its own proprietary products, think about how that would affect the management of your personal portfolio. As for account minimums to open and to maintain an account, you need to be sure they fit your situation. For example, if the firm's minimum is $20 million and you have $2 million, unless the firm makes exceptions, you'll have to eliminate it from your list of possibilities.

Item 3. "Fees, Costs, Conflicts, and Standard of Conduct"

Item 3 packs a great deal of information about firms through nine subsections (and two "conversation starters," which are discussed in the next chapter).

Item 3 (Continued): Fees

Starting with *"What fees will I pay?"*[11] this section calls for a discussion of "Principal Fees and Costs," and the "conflicts of interest they create."[12] This is the first item that mentions conflicts. As you read ahead, make a note of how the SEC wants different firms to report conflicts, especially in connection with the financial incentives firms and their representatives must report. As you read through the differences in required disclosures, you'll start to see how incentives differentiate firms.

Investment advisers would describe ongoing asset-based fees (or other fixed fees, wrap fee program fees, or direct fee arrangements). The CRS

---

10. *Id.* CRS Instructions for Item 2(B)(iv).
11. *Id.* at 12. CRS Instructions for Item 3(A).
12. *Id.* CRS Instructions for Item 3(A)(i).

instructions provide an example for those who charge an asset-based fee to explain the potential conflict as follows:

> The more assets there are in a retail investor's advisory account, the more a retail investor will pay in fees, and the firm may therefore have an *incentive to encourage the retail investor to increase the assets in his or her account.*[13]

For broker-dealers, transaction-based fees would be described. The instructions to the CRS provide this example of conflicts disclosure for transaction-based fees:

> A retail investor would be charged more when there are more trades in his or her account, and that the firm may therefore have an *incentive to encourage a retail investor to trade often.*[14]

Note: Compare the two preceding descriptions. In each case, there are conflicts. In the adviser environment, the incentive is to encourage you to "increase the assets" in your account; in the broker-dealer environment, the incentive is to encourage you to "trade often." It is important that you consider which environment might be more desirable for you or your spouse or partner.

Item 3 (Continued): Description of Other Fees and Costs

Next under Item 3 is a "Description of Other Fees and Costs,"[15] which expands the first section to include "fees and costs the retail investor will pay directly or indirectly." Note the word "indirectly." Examples are custodian fees, accountant maintenance fees, fees related to mutual funds and variable annuities, transaction fees, and product-level fees. Again, the best way (perhaps the only way) to see the impact of these disclosures is to compare firms.

---

13. *Id.* CRS Instructions for Item 3(A)(i)(b)(2) (emphasis added).
14. *Id.* CRS Instructions for Item 3(A)(i) (emphasis added).
15. *Id.* CRS Instructions for Item 3(A)(ii).

Item 3 (Continued): Additional Information

Then, comes "Additional Information,"[16] which mandates this language for all firms:

> You will pay fees and costs whether you make or lose money on your investments. Fees and costs will reduce any amount of money you make on your investments over time. Please make sure you understand what fees and costs you are paying.[17]

Note: When comparing firms to retain for personal portfolio management, return to fees and costs after digesting legal obligations and standards of conduct, which come next.

Item 3 (Continued): Standards of Conduct

Next in Item 3 are "Standards of Conduct,"[18] which vary by the type of firm. This is mandated language by type of firm.

- If you are a broker-dealer, use the heading: "What are your legal obligations to me *when providing recommendations*? How else does your firm make money and what conflicts of interest do you have?"
- If you are an investment adviser, use the heading: "What are your legal obligations to me *when acting as my investment adviser*? How else does your firm make money and what conflicts of interest do you have?"
- If you are a dual registrant that prepares a single relationship summary, use the heading: "What are your legal obligations to me *when providing recommendations as my broker-dealer or when acting as my investment adviser*? How else does your firm make money and what conflicts of interest do you have?"[19]

---

16. *Id.* at 13. CRS Instructions for Item 3(A)(iii).
17. *Id.* CRS Instructions for Item 3(A)(iii).
18. *Id.* CRS Instructions for Item 3(B)(i).
19. *Id.* CRS Instructions for Item 3(B) (emphasis added).

Item 3 (Continued): Best Interest

All three types of firms (stand-alone broker-dealer, stand-alone investment adviser, and dual registrant) must make a mandated "best interest" statement. However, best interest has different meanings depending on whether the firm is regulated under the 1934 Act or the Advisers Act. (See Chapter 10 for a discussion of these standards.) For now, let me point out a few differentiating points that the CRS calls out.

Notice that the first statement (below) refers to "acting as investment adviser" and "investment advice." The second, which is almost identical, applies to brokers and refers to "recommendations." This reinforces one difference between brokers and advisers, based on the service they provide (recommendations versus investment advice).

An investment adviser must include this statement:

> When *we act as your investment adviser*, we have to act in your *best interest* and not put our interest ahead of yours. At the same time, the way we make money creates some conflicts with your interests. You should understand and ask us about these conflicts because they can affect *the investment advice we provide you.*[20]

A broker must provide the following statement if it provides recommendations:

> When we provide you with a *recommendation*, we have to act in your *best interest* and not put our interest ahead of yours. At the same time, the way we make money creates some conflicts with your interests. You should understand and ask us about these conflicts because they can affect the recommendations we provide you.[21]

A dual registrant must provide the following statement if it provides recommendations and prepares a single CRS instead of two (two are optional for dual registrants):

---

20. *Id.* at 14. CRS Instructions for Item 3(B)(i)(b) (emphasis added).
21. *Id.* at 13–14. CRS Instructions for Item 3(B)(i)(a) (emphasis added).

When we provide you with a *recommendation* as your broker-dealer or act as your *investment adviser,* we have to act in your *best interest* and not put our interest ahead of yours. At the same time, the way we make money creates some conflicts with your interests. You should understand and ask us about these conflicts because they can affect the recommendations and investment advice we provide you.[22]

The CRS calls for examples. You will want to study them and compare them to other firms' CRSs. Refer also to the discussion of conflicts in Chapter 11.

Item 3 (Continued): Making Money and Conflicts

Next, the CRS must describe examples of conflicts imbedded in the firm's way of doing business. "Examples of Ways You Make Money and Conflicts of Interest."[23]

Specifically, firms are instructed to summarize the following ways in which *they* and *their affiliates* make money on their services and investments. Firms must explain the *incentives* created by each of the following four situations.[24]

- Proprietary Products: Investments that are issued, sponsored, or managed by [the firm] or [its] affiliates.[25]
- Third-Party Payments: Compensation [the firm] receive[s] from third parties when [the firm] recommend[s] or sell[s] certain investments.[26]
- Revenue Sharing: Investments where the manager or sponsor of those investments or another third party (such as an intermediary) shares "with [the firm] revenue it earns on those investments."[27]

22. *Id.* at 14. CRS Instructions for Item 3(B)(i)(c) (emphasis added).
23. *Id.* CRS Instructions for Item 3(B)(ii).
24. *Id.* CRS Instructions for Item 3(B)(ii).
25. *Id.* at 15. CRS Instructions for Item 3(B)(ii)(a).
26. *Id.* CRS Instructions for Item 3(B)(ii)(b).
27. *Id.* CRS Instructions for Item 3(B)(ii)(c).

- Principal Trading: Investments [the firm] buy[s] from a retail investor, and/or investments [the firm] sell[s] to a retail investor, for or from [the firm's] own accounts, respectively.[28]

Note: Each of these conflicts is recognized by regulators as an area that investors need to address when assessing a possible firm–client relationship. These four enumerated conflicts are not unusual in the financial services industry, particularly with large organizations that have multiple lines of business. Your job will be to determine your sensitivity to conflicts as you prepare for decades of retirement investing. How to do that is the subject of Chapter 14.

As you review Form CRS, you will find some firms with *none* of these enumerated conflicts, which again, can help narrow choices. In fact, some firms have been organized with the intent to do business with as few conflicts as possible. Can a firm have *no* conflicts? As discussed in Chapter 11, that simply isn't possible. As a result, the instructions call for the firm to summarize at least one material conflict of interest in the CRS. The CRS provides this example:

The more assets you have in the advisory account, including cash, the more you will pay us. We therefore have an incentive to increase the assets in your account in order to increase our fees.[29]

Increasing assets occurs in two ways: (1) your adviser makes money for you that increased the assets through performance, and (2) your adviser encourages you to bring additional assets into the sphere of the firm's management.

---

28. *Id.* CRS Instructions for Item 3(B)(ii)(d).

29. Annex B: Form CRS Mock-up—Stand-alone Investment Adviser, U.S. Sec. & Exch. Comm'n (2018), https://www.sec.gov/news/statements/2018/annex-b-3-ia-reg istrant-mock-up.pdf (emphasis added).

Item 3 (Continued): Making Money

"How do your financial professionals make money?"[30]

Under this section, the firm must summarize how its "financial professionals are compensated, including cash and non-cash compensation, and the conflicts of interest those payments create."[31] The firm must include whether the firm's financial professionals are paid based on these types of factors:

- the amount of client assets they service;
- the time and complexity required to meet a client's needs;
- the product sold (i.e., differential compensation);
- product sales commissions; or
- revenue the firm earns from the financial professional's advisory services or recommendations.[32]

The way a firm compensates representatives will show you whether you are working with a commissioned salesperson who could be incentivized by production quotas or could benefit from selling a certain type of product over another.

For example, this is a dual registrant's CRS disclosure:

How do your financial professionals make money? Most of our Financial Advisors receive a percentage of the revenue that they generate from our services, which includes transaction-based fees, investment advisory fees, trails and referral fees. The percentage increases as the level of revenue a Financial Advisor generates for [the firm] increases (known as production). Financial Advisors are also eligible to receive financial and recognition awards based on their:

- Production
- Length of service with [the firm]
- New business they generate. . .

---

30. Form CRS Relationship Summary: Amendments to Form ADV, *supra* note 5, at 15. CRS Instructions for Item 3(C).

31. *Id.* CRS Instructions for Item 3(C)(i).

32. *Id.* CRS Instructions for Item 3(C)(ii).

We and our Financial Advisors also receive non-cash compensation from certain product sponsors that can include occasional gifts, meals, tickets and/or other entertainment, sponsorship of educational or training events, including educational events Financial Advisors arrange for clients and prospective clients.[33]

What should you see in this disclosure? Again, to get context, you need to compare firms. Here are a few more. First, is another dual registrant's incentive disclosure.

Incentive compensation is calculated and paid annually based on individual and company performance and is *not* directly linked to sales, existing assets or differentiation among products, other than as one of many factors in company performance. Incentive plans are designed to encourage registered representatives to establish and maintain strong customer relationships, to align with their long-term interests and provide them with the best possible service.[34]

Compare a stand-alone adviser's disclosure.

All of our financial professionals are paid a salary as employees of [the firm] and may receive a discretionary bonus annually. Certain new professionals of [the firm] may also receive compensation for the acquisition of new clients.[35]

As you can see, these disclosures help one get an understanding of the culture of the firm. It pays to compare and contrast, and to start to collect some criteria for selecting a firm to manage your money.

---

33. Form CRS: Relationship Summary for Individual UBS Wealth Management Clients (UBS, NY, 2021), 1, https://www.ubs.com/content/dam/assets/wma/us/shared/documents/relationship-summary.pdf

34. Form CRS: Customer Relationship Summary for American Century Investments®, MO, 2020, 3, https://www.americancentury.com/content/direct/en/legal/relationship-details.html (emphasis added).

35. Firm E: ADV, Part 3 (Client Relationship Summary), 2022. ADV accessed February 23, 2022.

Note: As you read through this discussion, I expect you will formulate your own views on what is and is not important to you personally. Part IV of the book will help you do that.

Item 4. Disciplinary History

"Do you or your financial professionals have legal or disciplinary history?"[36]

This item requires disclosure of the legal or disciplinary history of the firm and "any" of its financial professionals. The types of matters that are reportable are:

- Disciplinary information in your Form ADV[37] . . .
- Legal or disciplinary history in your Form BD[38]. . .
- Disclosures for any of your financial professionals in [Forms U4, U5, and U6].[39]

If the firm *does* have disclosable legal or disciplinary history, the firm is limited to saying "yes" in its CRS. No explanation is permissible, only a "yes" or "no."

No matter the response, the CRS must state: "Visit Investor.gov for a free and simple search tool to research our firm and our financial professionals." Investor.gov is the SEC's Office of Investor Education and Advocacy site. That site does not take you directly to the disclosure you need to read. To find that, enter the name of the firm in the "Check Out Your Investment Professional" search box.[40]

36. Form CRS Relationship Summary: Amendments to Form ADV, *supra* note 5, at 16. CRS Instructions for Item 4.

37. Form ADV (Item 11 of Part 1A or Item 9 of Part 2A).

38. Form BD (Items 11 A–K) (except to the extent such information is not released to BrokerCheck, pursuant to FINRA Rule 8312). © 2022 FINRA. All rights reserved. FINRA is a registered trademark of the Financial Industry Regulatory Authority, Inc. Reprinted with permission from FINRA.

39. Items 14 A–M on Form U4 (Uniform Application for Securities Industry Registration or Transfer); Items 7A or 7C–F of Form U5 (Uniform Termination Notice for Securities Industry Registration); Form U6 (Uniform Disciplinary Action Reporting Form) (except to the extent such information is not released to BrokerCheck, pursuant to FINRA Rule 8312).

40. Information presented on www.sec.gov is considered public information and may be copied or further distributed by users of the web site without the SEC's permission.

Alternatively, you can go to Investor.gov/CRS and click on "How do I find a firm's or individual's disciplinary history?" You'll be instructed to use the "search tool,"[41] where you would select "firm" or "individual." After you insert the name, if the words "Disclosure Reported" appear, the individual (or firm) has disciplinary history that you need to read about.[42]

Next, click on the button for "Get Details." A brokerage firm's disciplinary history will be under the heading "Disclosures." For an investment adviser, you will have to click on the "Part 2 Brochures" and link to the "Disciplinary Information." When you look up a dual registrant, you will find two "get details" boxes, one for the "registered investment adviser firm" and one for the "brokerage firm." You will need to read both.

When looking up a representative, you'll look up the individual by name, then click the link to "Get Full Report." Disciplinary history will be under the heading "Disclosures."

Once you view one firm's Detailed Report, you can easily compare it to another firm's Detailed Report. What to make of the information you find will depend on you and your sensitivity to adviser risk, which we return to in Chapter 15.

Note: These disclosures are required reading for anyone who acts in the fiduciary capacity, as a lawyer does, when referring someone to a financial firm. They make it easy to judge whether a firm with many disclosures is worth retaining.

Item 5. Additional Information[43]

In this section of the CRS, the firm lets you know where you can find more information about the subject matter of the CRS. As we discussed

---

41. The search tool is easily missed, since the tool is located in a box at the bottom of the page. The box is called "Check Out Your Investment Professional." As an alternative, you can use BrokerCheck at https://brokercheck.finra.org/, © 2022 FINRA. All rights reserved. FINRA is a registered trademark of the Financial Industry Regulatory Authority, Inc. Reprinted with permission from FINRA.

42. "Welcome to Investor.gov/CRS," Investor.gov, U.S. Sec. & Exch. Comm'n, 2022, https://www.investor.gov/CRS.

43. Form CRS Relationship Summary: Amendments to Form ADV, *supra* note 5, at 16.

in the last chapter, for an investment adviser (and a dual registrant), there is the Form ADV and ADV Part 2A (also called the "Brochure"), both of which are filed with the SEC and available on the SEC's website (adviser info.sec.gov). You can also start at BrokerCheck[44] (you will be redirected to adviserinfo.sec.gov).

For a stand-alone broker-dealer (and a dual registrant), you'll look for Form BD, which you will find on the sec.gov site, the Best Interest Disclosure (new for 2020) (available on the firm's website), and the "Detailed Report" (available on BrokerCheck). In Appendix C, I'll take you through how to find information using BrokerCheck.

Key Takeaways

The Form CRS is an indispensable resource that allows you to easily compare financial firms and choose the one that is best for you. The review process is a "compare and contrast" exercise, comparing one firm's CRS to another's.

The review can tell you:

- Whether the firm you're considering provides the type of services you need
- What conflicts of interest the firm and representative might have
- Whether a firm or representative has a disciplinary history

To really understand the differences in regulation and the impact on you, the investor, revisit Chapter 11 on conflicts of interest. Next, we'll talk about how to interview a representative.

---

44. https://brokercheck.finra.org/. © 2022 FINRA. All rights reserved. FINRA is a registered trademark of the Financial Industry Regulatory Authority, Inc. Reprinted with permission from FINRA.

Chapter 13
Let's Talk: The SEC's "Conversation Starters" and More

After considering the type of firm you will likely want to retain, you'll want to interview the firm's representative who would be your primary contact to implement your investment strategy. This chapter will prepare you for that talk. The goal is to make sure that your mutual interests are aligned.

Keep in mind that when you meet with potential candidates, they are representing the firm that employs them. Your interview needs to encompass questions about both the firm and the individual who represents the firm, your "financial professional." For this purpose, the SEC provides a list of questions for you to ask that are incorporated into the firm's CRS (discussed in the last chapter). Let's start with the list of questions provided in the CRS and, then, let's put them into context with some commentary and additional questions.

Conversation Starters

Part of the mandated language of the CRS is a series of questions the SEC calls "Conversation Starters." These are questions that the SEC would like you pose to the financial professional you are interested in possibly retaining. You will also want your current representative to answer these questions, especially if you are transitioning into retirement with its set of new investment goals.

The following conversation starters are quoted verbatim from the CRS instructions. *I have numbered them for convenience.* The first three ask the same question in different contexts, as you will see, distinguishing between broker-dealers, investment advisers, and dual registrants.

1. For stand-alone broker-dealers: "Given my financial situation, should I choose a brokerage service? Why or why not?"

2. For stand-alone investment advisers: "Given my financial situation, should I choose an investment advisory service? Why or why not?"

3. For dual registrants: "Given my financial situation, should I choose an investment advisory service? Should I choose a brokerage service? Should I choose both types of services? Why or why not?"

Questions 4 through 9 do not distinguish between types of firms. Question 10 returns to firms, as it leads to the type of person who might supervise the representative (whether an adviser or a broker).

Notice that questions 4 through 9 dive into the role of the representative and elicit background information, some of which you might be hesitant to ask on your own initiative, such as those dealing with "relevant qualifications" (question 5), conflicts (question 8), and disciplinary history (question 9).

4. "How will you choose investments to recommend to me?"

5. "What is your relevant experience, including your licenses, education, and other qualifications? What do these qualifications mean?"

6. "Help me understand how these fees and costs (described in the CRS; see Chapter 12) might affect my investments."

7. "If I give you $10,000 to invest, how much will go to fees and costs, and how much will be invested for me?"

8. "How might your conflicts of interest affect me, and how will you address them?"

9. "As a financial professional, do you have any disciplinary history? For what type of conduct?"

10. "Who is my primary contact person? Is he or she a representative of an investment adviser or a broker-dealer? Who can I talk to if I have concerns about how this person is treating me?"[1]

---

1. Form CRS Relationship Summary: Amendments to Form ADV, U.S. Sec. & Exch. Comm'n, 17 C.F.R. § 249.640 (2019) 11–17, https://www.sec.gov/rules/final/2019/34-86 032-appendix-b.pdf.

Note: Depending on your sensitivity to "adviser risk," you'll either focus on or ignore questions that frame the relationship, namely 8 (conflicts) and 9 (disciplinary history). Based on my decades of personal experience, I would rank these higher than the other questions.

While these questions are intended to be asked orally, a few firms have published their answers.[2] Most have not, which means you will need to take time to discuss them with the firm's representative.

Tell Me About Your Firm

You'll want to know how the firm (whether a stand-alone broker, stand-alone adviser, or a dual registrant) describes the services it offers. This picks up Conversation Starter questions 1, 2, 3, as well as 4, 6, and 7, which deal with fees.

To get the answers you need to prepare for retirement, I would like to have you discuss how the firm expects to manage your retirement portfolio to meet your needs for cash flow during your lifetime as well as your legacy interests.

To give you a good answer, the response has to take into consideration your goals, how to customize a portfolio to meet your objectives, and how the firm will supervise and monitor your portfolio. You'll want to hear how the firm assesses your current holdings and goals before making a recommendation of any sort. Likewise, you'll want to know how the firm defines the demands that will be placed on the portfolio if there is a retirement income gap. What about doing a cash flow analysis? And, importantly, what does the firm do about monitoring your portfolio regularly? How does the firm explain its selling discipline (when to sell a holding)? How does the firm define and address risk?

---

2. Read Vanguard's "Form CRS Conversation Starters" for its advisory business here https://personal.vanguard.com/pdf/formcrsDA_061020.pdf and for its brokerage customers here https://personal.vanguard.com/pdf/CRSFAQ.pdf.

Read Betterment's Form CRS Conversation Starters at https://www.betterment.com/legal/form-crs-overview/.

> **Note:** It is crucial that the firm demonstrates that it is working with your unique set of assets, goals, and liabilities, as opposed to trying to fit you into a cookie cutter solution (or product sale).

You would be looking for clues about (1) whether the firm indeed shoulders the responsibility of managing customized portfolios for clients, (2) the standard of care to which the firm is held under the law (best interest fiduciary for ongoing management or best interest at the time of the recommendation—point of sale), and (3) your fit into that service model (do you direct investment choices; are investments made by the firm under a discretionary contract, etc.).

Be alert to culture. If the firm's process is offering a financial product or managed account solution too early, you may be dealing with a firm that prioritizes sales over portfolio management.

What About Financial Incentives?

Conversation Starter 8 is: "How might your conflicts of interest affect me, and how will you address them?"

You are looking for a statement of the conflict followed by how it is resolved. As an example, this is a written response to this question. Notice the italicized conflict, the "financial incentive" and how it is addressed (italicized).

> We also have a financial incentive to recommend you invest in the service offering from which we expect to earn greater revenue. For example, we have a *financial incentive* to recommend our Premium offering, for which we charge a 0.40% annual fee, to current Digital clients, whom we charge a 0.25% annual fee. *We seek to address this conflict by ensuring that our financial consultants do not receive higher compensation for recommending Premium over Digital.*[3]

The representative needs to be forthcoming and responsive about the conflicts noted in the CRS itself, such as proprietary products, third-party payments, revenue sharing, or principal trading in Form CRS—and his or

---

3. Betterment Form CRS, https://www.betterment.com/legal/form-crs-overview.

her own conflicts, which are most easily identified by financial incentives. (Revisit Chapter 11 on conflicts and Chapter 12 on Form CRS.)

Are There Disciplinary Disclosures?

The Conversation Starter that I've numbered 9 is: "As a financial professional, do you have any disciplinary history? For what type of conduct?"

If the representative does have disciplinary disclosures, you need to check his or her BrokerCheck record and search disciplinary disclosures of the firm itself as well. See Appendix C.

What should you make of the response if there is disciplinary history? Should you continue your due diligence on that particular firm and representatives or move on to another? If you are motivated to work with that individual notwithstanding disclosures, that's your call.

On the other hand, if you are making a referral to that individual, consider your due diligence responsibilities. If you want to understand the nature of the disciplinary action, the start is learning about the types of actions that call for disclosure, namely those required in Forms U4, U5, and U6.[4]

Two More Questions

The two remaining Conversation Starters (5 and 10) I put last, but not because they are less important.

Five is: "What is your relevant experience, including your licenses, education, and other qualifications? What do these qualifications mean?" Ten is: "Who is my primary contact person? Is he or she a representative of an investment adviser or a broker-dealer? Who can I talk to if I have concerns about how this person is treating me?"

When asking the representative about "relevant experience" and "qualifications," I'm interested in hearing about the types of clients (assets, ages, investment goals) he or she is skilled at handling. I would want to know if he or she prepares an IPS (Chapter 6), who does the

---

4. Items 14 A–M on Form U4 (Uniform Application for Securities Industry Registration or Transfer); Items 7A or 7C–F of Form U5 (Uniform Termination Notice for Securities Industry Registration); Form U6 (Uniform Disciplinary Action Reporting Form) (except to the extent such information is not released to BrokerCheck, pursuant to FINRA Rule 8312).

Form CRS Relationship Summary: Amendments to Form ADV, *supra* note 1, at 16.

work for you to develop a retirement strategy, and who determines how it is to be implemented.

I'd also ask about the representative's typical week and typical day and his or her production requirements and payout grid. Are you looking for a representative who is a top producer (translation: top salesperson)? Or, are you looking for a representative who works for a firm that limits compensation to salaries and bonuses based on client service as opposed to meeting sales goals? Both options are available to you.

I also want to know the employment history of the representative. How many firms has he or she been associated with over time and what types of firms were they? I'd like to know about the circumstances behind changing firms, no matter how many were involved, a few or many.[5]

If the person has been recruited to the current firm with a recruitment bonus arrangement, you would want to know the details, especially if you followed the representative to his or her new firm. Recruitment arrangements can pose conflicts, as discussed by FINRA in "5 Questions to Ask When Your Broker Changes Firms."[6]

More specifically, when a new firm recruits your representative, a recruiting bonus may be involved. The bonus may be tied to a loan that is forgivable[7] over time if and only if the representative meets production requirements (translation: meets sales quotas).

---

5. A quick search on BrokerCheck can be revealing. As an example, a recent search for a particular broker showed an employment history with 14 firms in 19 years and four disciplinary disclosures.

6. See FINRA's "5 Questions to Ask When Your Broker Changes Firms," at https://www.finra.org/investors/learn-to-invest/brokerage-accounts/5-questions-ask-when-your-broker-changes-firms. Quoting from that source: "Could financial incentives create a conflict of interest for your broker? In general, you should discuss the reasons your broker decided to change firms. Some firms pay brokers financial incentives when they join, which could include bonuses based on customer assets the broker brings in, incentives for selling in-house products or a higher share of commissions. Similarly, some firms pay financial incentives to retain brokers or customers. While there's nothing wrong with these incentives in either case, they can create a conflict of interest for the broker. Whether you stay or go, you should carefully consider whether your broker's advice is aligned with your investment strategy and goals." © 2022 FINRA. All rights reserved. FINRA is a registered trademark of the Financial Industry Regulatory Authority, Inc. Reprinted with permission from FINRA.

7. See *Why Broker-Dealer Forgivable Notes Aren't (Really) Forgiven and Are Instead Ultimately Paid Back By Clients*, Kitces.com (Nov. 23, 2020, 7:02 AM), https://www

The following quote is an example of an especially clear and well-crafted best interest disclosure document explaining that recruits "typically" receive financial incentives and what that might mean to a client of the recruit.[8]

Compensation for Financial Advisors recruited from other firms

Financial Advisors recruited from another firm typically receive financial incentives for joining [the Firm] and on an ongoing basis. These payments can be substantial and take various forms, including salary guarantees, loans, transition bonus payments and various forms of compensation to encourage Financial Advisors to join [the Firm], and are also contingent on your Financial Advisor's continued employment. Therefore, even if the fees you pay at [the Firm] remain the same or are less, the transfer of your assets to [the Firm] contribute to your Financial Advisor's ability to meet such targets and to receive additional compensation even if not directly related to your account or the fees you pay to us. *These practices create an incentive and a conflict of interest* for your Financial Advisor to recommend the transfer of your account assets to [the Firm] since a significant part of the Financial Advisor's compensation is often contingent on the Financial Advisor achieving a pre-determined level of revenue and/or assets at [the Firm]. You should carefully consider whether your Financial Advisor's advice is aligned with your investment strategy and goals.[9]

A "significant part" of the recruit's revenue often depends on hitting revenue goals—including revenue from your accounts if you move with the representative to the new firm. The target production is based on the accounts the recruit is successful at transferring to the new firm. You'll want to know what happens if the recruit fails to live up to the bargain.

.kitces.com/blog/forgivable-note-gdc-recruiting-bonus-broker-dealer-fiduciary-friendly-embedded-costs-revenue-sharing-markups-fees/.

8. Your Relationship with UBS: Understanding Our Approach, Services, Fees, Compensation and Conflicts of Interest 13, UBS, June 2021, https://www.ubs.com/content/dam/assets/wma/us/shared/documents/relationship-with-ubs.pdf.

9. *Id.* at 15 (emphasis added).

Asking about production requirements that might impact you is a natural part of the investigative process. You can find this information in the best interest disclosure documents of dual registrants. You may also find an SEC cease-and-desist proceeding to shed more light on the conflict.[10]

Note: Very simply, any person who has a representative, needs to understand production requirements, as they pose conflicts of interest between the representatives and the client; prudence dictates such a review, as all potential conflicts must be understood and accepted (or averted by choosing another type of business model).

If your current representative leaves and you decide to stay with the firm, you will likely be assigned a new representative. Be sure to interview him or her as we've discussed in this chapter. Add a question about whether the new representative follows the methods and protocols of your current representative.

Note: Consider whether you want a firm that applies a set process and protocol for managing portfolios under a long-standing rule set. Consider that the methodology continues whether or not an individual representative stays or leaves.

Supervisor

As to question 10, it is a very good idea to get the name of a supervisor. In the event of any misunderstandings between the representative and you, you will turn to the supervisor for help. Notice that the question distinguishes between representatives of brokerage firms and advisers. Supervisory responsibilities differ based on the distinctions in the laws governing advisers and brokers, as we've discussed in Chapters 9 and 10.

---

10. Firm F: U.S. Securities and Exchange Commission Cease-and-Desist Order, 2021. (Failure to disclose forgivable loans and related conflicts of interest.)

Key Takeaways

Anticipating that you will be interviewing representatives of different types of firms, the SEC's Conversation Starters are an effective way to confirm your understanding of the services you can expect to receive and the standards of care that will apply to the relationship. Certain of the questions (namely disciplinary matters and conflicts) will also give you a sense of the firm and the person when it comes to compliance with the law. Taken together with the CRS, this exercise will help you ascertain the type of environment and service you will want for yourself.

It might be helpful to review Chapter 11's examples of conflicts and financial incentives to prepare for the dialogue.

PART IV
Portfolio Management Gets Personal

In this, the last part of the book, I'd like to return to this basic premise—that retirement investing calls for a big picture strategic approach that goes beyond stock picking to portfolio management. That management function is the realm of investment advisers (whether they be stand-alone firms or dual registrants).

As former SEC Chairman Jay Clayton explained:

> Do you want someone *managing your account on an ongoing basis* based on your broad financial goals and needs and movements in the markets? If so, *an investment adviser* may be best for you. . . .
>
> Or do you plan to buy a few stocks, bonds, mutual funds or ETFs and hold them for the long term with a few adjustments over the years? In that case, a broker[-dealer] may be best for you.[1]

Because the management of a retirement portfolio is more than a simple tactical exercise of what stocks to buy, investors are faced with a dilemma. Status quo bias leads to wanting to sit tight, making no changes.

For all the reasons we discussed, prudence and logic tell us that change may be necessary. However, self-discovery precedes the shift if there is to be one.

---

1. *Brokers & Advisers—Which Is Right For Me*, YOUTUBE, 1:47, (Aug. 15, 2019), https://www.youtube.com/watch?v=PX-WXjTw5OY (emphasis added).

As we discussed in Parts I and II, reviewing your needs and goals in light of how the markets work comes first. Then, comes the assessment of financial service firms that could provide investment management services appropriate for a retirement portfolio (Part III).

Now, it's time to marry the two. The next chapter will help you devise your own set of standards in choosing a representative of a firm, again, whether he or she is with a stand-alone adviser or a dual registrant. Chapter 14, Introducing the "Know Your Representative" Rule, will help you formulate a personal set of guidelines based on factors *you* deem important.

And, finally, in the last chapter of the book (Chapter 15, The Future Is Yours: What Will You Do Next?), I'll provide a self-assessment tool that will help you decide what to review before making any changes or deciding on status quo. This last chapter will guide you as you formulate next steps.

Chapter 14
Introducing the "Know Your Representative" Rule

When you arrive at a decision about the type of firm you want to retain, next, you'll need to get clarity on how to choose a "representative" of that firm.[1] I've thought long and hard about how to make this process both effective and efficient. The goal is to help you apply what we've discussed into a rule set that is personally meaningful to you.

I've modeled my approach on the brokerage industry's "Know Your Customer" (KYC) rule. The KYC rule calls for the broker to use "reasonable due diligence" when opening and maintaining an account for a customer.[2]

I like the idea of you, the investor, applying a comparable "Know Your Representative" (KYR) rule. Your KYR rule would call for reasonable due diligence before you engage a representative to act as your personal portfolio manager.[3] The rule could be used with any type of firm, but the application of the rule would differ somewhat depending on whether you

---

1. For purposes of this discussion, I am not distinguishing between "investment adviser representatives" of Registered Investment Advisers regulated under the Advisers Act and "registered representatives" of brokerage firms regulated under the 1934 Act.

2. *2090. Know Your Customer Rule*, Finra.org, FINRA, 2012, www.finra.org/rules -guidance/rulebooks/finra-rules/2090

FINRA Rule 2090 Know Your Customer: "Every [FINRA] member shall use reasonable diligence, in regard to the opening and maintenance of every account, to know (and retain) the essential facts concerning every customer."

Supplementary Material: "For purposes of this Rule, facts 'essential' to 'knowing the customer' are those required to (a) effectively service the customer's account, (b) act in accordance with any special handling instructions for the account, (c) understand the authority of each person acting on behalf of the customer, and (d) comply with applicable laws, regulations, and rules." © 2022 FINRA. All rights reserved. FINRA is a registered trademark of the Financial Industry Regulatory Authority, Inc. Reprinted with permission from FINRA.

3. Chapter 1.

were retaining an adviser who worked for a dual registrant or a stand-alone investment adviser. (That is, the business setting will be different, as we've discussed.)

The brokerage KYC rule looks to the ability to effectively service the customer's account; the KYR rule should focus on the representative being able to effectively service *your portfolio needs*. To prepare, we need to look at the business practices you can encounter as a client of an investment adviser, broker-dealer, or dual registrant. With that background, you can see whether you could benefit from a KYR rule as a foundation for reasonable due diligence, using the CRS (Chapter 12) as a tool and the Conversation Starters that are included in the CRS (Chapter 13).

Based on my experience with investors, I'm going to anticipate that your views on due diligence will differ from anyone else's. Some people will be keen to avoid any representatives who work for firms that have disciplinary disclosures; others will be more forgiving. Some will want to carefully review how the representative earns money; others won't care at all about whether there are incentives.

The goal is to develop a few simple KYR rules that encompass what is important *to you* in the retirement phase of your investment life. The rules flow from your personal assessment of what you want in a representative.

KYR Assessment

The KYR assessment focuses on just a few things: expertise, performance, management of a retirement portfolio, culture, and compensation. All of these topics are subjects we've discussed in detail in the book. We're leaving out the straightforward elements, such as the service offerings, office location, and the like. You would assign a rating to each item based on how important the matter is to you in a relationship, as follows: A=Desirable; B=No opinion; C=Undesirable; D=Deal breaker. The difference between the last two is intensity.

This KYR assessment is such a personal exercise that I will refrain from telling you what I would do (but, by now, you might guess). Here are the categories:

Expertise. The representative's expertise with retirement portfolios. What are the elements? You will need to define the service you want and need first, based on Parts I and II of the book. Then, see if you can match those requirements to the representative. Rating: A, B, C, D?

Performance. The representative's method of assessing performance for a retirement portfolio. What are the elements? How is performance defined for a retirement portfolio? Is your retirement income gap covered now and will it be in the future as needs change, and inflation and taxes affect outcomes? What about meeting capital appreciation goals? What about the risk assumed to meet those goals? What about targets and indices? What are the metrics used? (Discussed in Part II.) Rating: A, B, C, D?

Management of a Retirement Portfolio. The representative's method of managing your retirement portfolio. What are the elements? Do the methods follow a protocol that is well defined, time tested, and repeatable? Are the methodologies used by the representative unique to him or her? Or do they reflect a protocol that is firm-run or team-run? Is there an Investment Policy Statement that directs the management of the portfolio? What types of reports are provided on a regular basis? (Discussed in Parts I, II, and III.) Rating: A, B, C, D?

Culture. The culture or environment of the firm the representative works for. What are the elements? Type of firm, based on regulation and standards of care, disclosed conflicts and disclosed disciplinary matters. (Discussed in Part III). Founder's vision: sales culture vs. service culture? Retail shop vs. boutique? Rating: A, B, C, D?

Compensation. The representative's compensation. What are the elements? What are you paying directly and indirectly and how does that translate into compensation for the representative? How else does the representative make money? (Discussed in Part III). Does how the representative make money incentivize him or her in any way when it comes to advising you? Rating: A, B, C, D?

Rating Results

This is how the rating system might be used.

If the representative has no expertise in retirement investing, you might rate experience a D (Deal breaker) especially if you fall within the demographics laid out in Chapter 1 (for example, having a retirement income gap and limited time or interest in managing the portfolio yourself). That would disqualify that representative and you would move on.

But, what if the representative happens to be your brother-in-law? Would you adjust the D rating to an A (Desirable)? Unlikely. What about a B for No opinion or a C for Undesirable? If you are honest with yourself, a C or D is the right rating. That perspective will give you a chance to say, I'm willing to give expertise less weight in the overall scheme of things since there might be other benefits to dealing with my brother-in-law. (Make sure to make a note of those other benefits.)

What about disciplinary matters? If the representative has five disciplinary disclosures, you would likely rate him or her a D for Deal breaker and look for another representative. Would there be any reason to have a rating of A for Desirable (I can't think of any reason) or B for No opinion? What about C? (Not for me—what about you?) What if this representative is a life-long friend?

With the ratings, you'll be able to judge whether to eliminate someone from the running. Would one D lead you to say no? Would one C? You'll have to be the judge.

How to Use KYR Ratings

Your KYR rules will flow from your ratings.

For example, you might conclude that you are willing to accept a firm with a sales culture and conflicts of interest because you yourself expect to be vigilant and watchful. But you're not willing to accept a representative with disciplinary disclosures or someone who lacks both expertise in managing a retirement portfolio and clarity on how to measure performance.

On the other hand, you might find that the KYR assessment made you realize you would be satisfied with only A's—"Desirable" on all fronts considering the need for a trusted adviser for the decades of retirement that lie ahead.

Key Takeaways

Given that there is now much more transparency and clarity about the nature of services provided by financial firms and their representatives, there is a lot to learn about whether and how an individual can meet your expectations. The discovery process described here can lead to better informed decision making when you are considering a representative.

In the next and last chapter, we'll go through a self-assessment on the bigger issue of how to manage your portfolio in retirement.

Chapter 15
The Future Is Yours: What Will You Do Next?

As I said in the introduction to this book, my goal is for you to be able to feel *prepared* for retirement *on your own terms*. So far, we've discussed how to think of retirement in a way that allows for the development of a strategic plan to create a future that is uniquely yours. We also discussed resources at your disposal for retaining expertise to manage your portfolio, whether it is the firm you are currently working with or another . . . with the understanding that serving as your own investment adviser is always an option. And, in the last chapter, we addressed how to assess a representative based on your own personal criteria.

Now, the question is, what's next?

Lessons from Behavioral Economics

Behavioral economic theory tells us that we make *judgment errors* when faced with uncertainty, and there can be no greater uncertainty than transitioning from a career into retirement. "Status quo bias" (inertia)[1] can interfere when a change in direction is necessitated by transitions, such as the move into retirement with new portfolio objectives and new cash flow requirements.

Note: In behavioral economic terms, the greater the "past resource investment in a decision, the greater the inclination to continue the commitment in subsequent decisions."[2]

---

1. William Samuelson & Richard Zeckhauser, *Status Quo Bias in Decision Making*, 1(1) J. RISK & UNCERTAINTY 7-5 (1988), https://scholar.harvard.edu/files/rzeckhauser/files /status_quo_bias_in_decision_making.pdf.
2. *Id.* at 37.

Within that framework, let me pose a hypothetical situation: Put yourself in a fiduciary role for a moment. Assume that you are counseling Frank, who is about to retire from a career as a lawyer. His 401(k) is substantial. He and his wife, Franny, have no debt, having paid off the mortgage years ago. The children's tuition obligations are satisfied. Frank has a broker who does his investing. He has an accountant who does his taxes. He and Franny each have wills. What more do they need, if anything?

What's new in Frank's life? Frank has never retired before.

He has not attempted (yet) to conceptualize the future. There hasn't been any reason to do so. But now, something is changing in the calculus. His law firm earnings are terminating.

If asked, you might advise: "Why disrupt something that's been working for years? It's a lot easier to just let things be. Investing in retirement can't be all that different from what you're used to doing, right?"[3]

Or, perhaps you might say: "Retirement is a new venture for you. The paycheck needs to be replaced. Figure out how. Start with a personal situation audit; look at your numbers. Do the analysis. Engage expertise to complement your own know-how. That will give you the basis for creating a plan for lifetime financial security."

Which will it be? What advice might you give *yourself*?

To help you assess what actions you might take next, I've prepared a simple self-assessment based on what we've been discussing together.

15 Questions Lead to Setting Personal Priorities

The fifteen questions address separate and distinct points that we reviewed—each is a choice that only you can make (or not make)—no one else's responses will be relevant to you.

---

3. Franklin Templeton's Retirement Income Strategies and Expectations (RISE) 2021 survey studied stresses about financial security in retirement, https://www.franklintemple ton.com/forms-literature/download/REW-RISFL.

The goal of this self-analysis is to create a priority list for yourself. As you review the questions, you may need to refer to specific chapters for background; the footnote provides chapter references.[4]

See if any of these 15 questions are worth your time to explore. The rating system is: A=Essential; B=Important; C=Not worth the effort. For example, if you don't think it's worth your time to calculate your cash flow requirements in retirement, you would rate question 2 a "C." Instead, if you believe cash flows are essential to understand before making any investment decisions, your rating will be an "A."

1. Decide if you want to involve your spouse/partner in investment decisions in a way that creates a "joint venture" between the two of you. If so, decide how you would define responsibilities. Rating: A, B, or C?
2. Calculate your retirement cash flow requirements. Rating: A, B, or C?
3. Calculate your retirement income gap. Rating: A, B, or C?

4.

Question 1	Chapter 1
Question 2	Chapters 5, 7, 8
Question 3	Chapters 5, 7
Question 4	Chapter 7
Question 5	Chapter 7
Question 6	Chapter 6
Question 7	Chapter 8
Question 8	Chapters 11, 12, 13
Question 9	Chapters 9, 10
Question 10	Chapters 10, 11, 12
Question 11	Chapter 11
Question 12	Chapters 12, 13
Question 13	Chapters 11, 12
Question 14	Chapters 12, 13
Question 15	Chapters 6, 13

4. Decide on the method to use to fill the retirement income gap. (What methodology will be used to fund portfolio withdrawals?) Rating: A, B, or C?

5. Decide on strategic goals. For example, should goals include a plan to create a legacy for heirs and charity? Rating: A, B, or C?

6. Explore whether you want an Investment Policy Statement to set out your plan versus letting things unfold as time goes on instead. Rating: A, B, or C?

7. Explore performance measures and reports. Rating: A, B, or C?

8. Explore whether your current firm's services and culture align with your desires and needs in retirement. Rating: A, B, or C?

9. Explore legal standards of care. Does your firm's representative act as a fiduciary some of the time, all of the time, or none of the time? Rating: A, B, or C?

10. Explore conflicts of interest that you may come across and what to do about them. Rating: A, B, or C?

11. Decide whether it's worth searching for a firm that is close to conflict-free. Rating: A, B, or C?

12. Decide on the scope of your due diligence review of your current firm and any others that you are interested in. What will you do if there are disciplinary disclosures, regulatory sanctions, lawsuits, arbitrations? Rating: A, B, or C?

13. Decide if you want to review Form CRS for your current firm and other potential firms you might want to compare it to. Rating: A, B, or C?

14. Decide if you want to ask your current representative the CRS conversation starter questions. Rating: A, B, or C?

15. Explore if you need to expand your own skill set and knowledge base before engaging someone (or no one). Rating: A, B, or C?

This 15-point review identifies your personal priorities. Those you rate "A" you would tackle first, then "B." Those you rate "C" you would ignore. The time commitment for going through these details will depend on how well organized you are, the depth of your inquiry, and your interest in planning your retirement finances on your own or with the assistance of a trusted adviser. With this information, you can decide on next steps.

What to Make of Your Ratings: The Goal Is Choosing Wisely

The review should leave you with some impressions about what you are (and are not) willing to do. For example, you may decide that it is essential to calculate your retirement income gap, but you have *no* interest in an Investment Policy Statement.

Also consider revisiting the big-picture questions to ask yourself from Chapter 1, namely:

- Will my current methods of investing serve me well in my retirement, which will hopefully last decades, and serve my legacy goals thereafter?
- What more do I need to know to be successful when dealing with retirement finances?
- Do I want to be in charge of multiple accounts?
- How do I get reorganized as I move into retirement?
- If I have gaps in my knowledge, how can I identify expertise to fill those gaps?
- How do I measure success with a retirement portfolio?
- How do I avoid mistakes?
- How do I define my job as an investor in retirement?
- Can I, should I, delegate the role to someone else?

There is no better time than now to clarify your goals and capabilities so you can begin to develop a comprehensive retirement plan that will position you for success.

Key Takeaways

As we discussed in the introduction, retirement is a "critical juncture in an investor's life" . . . often accompanied with "irrevocable decisions."[5] When

---

5. Referencing the SEC Investor Advisory Committee's phraseology in *Regarding Proposed Regulation Best Interest, Form CRS, and Investment Advisers Act Fiduciary Guidance*, U.S. Securities and Exchange Commission's Investor Advisory Committee, Nov. 7, 2018, 4, https://www.sec.gov/spotlight/investor-advisory-committee-2012/recommendation-on-proposed-reg-bi.pdf.

unprepared, creating retirement income can be "the nastiest, hardest problem in finance" to solve[6]—but it doesn't have to be.

Preparation is the key. Take the time to identify your personal priorities. Then take a lawyer's point of view, and ask yourself: What can go wrong? What actions can be taken to avoid missteps?

Ultimately, you want to reach a comfort level knowing that you are making wise decisions that maximize your chances of a safe, secure, and healthy retirement, free from worries about finances . . . and if you are at all adventurous, to enjoy a "happy, wild and free"[7] retirement.

---

6. Barry Ritholtz, *Tackling the "Nastiest, Hardest Problem in Finance,"* Bloomberg Opinion, June 5, 2017, https://www.bloombergquint.com/onweb/tackling-the-nastiest -hardest-problem-in-finance. Also read Sharpe's "Retirement Income Analysis" (2019) at http://web.stanford.edu/~wfsharpe/RISMAT/.

7. Referencing Ernie Zelinski's book *How to Retire Happy, Wild, and Free*, who I should mention is also the author of *The Joy of Not Working*.

Epilogue
Your Role as Mentor, Coach and Role Model

In the many years that I have served as personal portfolio manager to my clients, I have had the privilege of learning from successful families. An observation is worth sharing. I've seen parents and grandparents teach younger people in their spheres to appreciate ethics and the value of learning, even in complex matters such as finance, investing, and the markets. Whether or not they intend to be, they are role models.

The same holds true for lawyers. As you engage in the personal portfolio management process, remember to share your insights with your colleagues and family. Younger lawyers and family members are watching you and learning from you. What a gift it is to serve as a coach or a role model a gift of time, knowledge, and wisdom.

If you would like to discuss anything we've reviewed together in this book, I welcome your questions, thoughts, and feedback. Please do e-mail me at julie@jacksongrant.us. In your subject line, mention that you read *The Discerning Investor.* Please also include your state of residence.

Appendix A
The Effect of Taxes When Withdrawing Monthly

Tables 3-1 through 3-7 in Chapter 3 assume no taxes are deducted during the holding period. However, even if the account is tax-deferred, withdrawals would trigger ordinary income at the investor's income tax rate each year. If the account were a Roth IRA, "qualified distributions"[1] would be tax-free.

To assess the effect of income taxes in a taxable account is complicated by the investor's particular tax situation. Yearly taxes would be triggered on dividends and capital gains distributions, as well as capital gains that are realized when withdrawals call for sales of positions. For that reason, it is difficult to model an after-tax effect. Results would vary based on the performance of the holdings on a month to month basis when withdrawals are made and whether they were fueled by income generated or sales of positions, depending on which tax lots were sold.

Understanding that modeling after-tax returns is unique to the individual taxpayer, Table A provides an illustration for a particular tax situation, using a hypothetical tool (Morningstar® Advisor Workstation^SM). The assumed federal income tax rate is 35%; capital gains tax rate is 15%; state tax rate is 6%, which are the tax rate assumptions for a single filer with gross income of $250,000.

Table A shows a before-tax and after-tax summary of Table 3-7, which is the longest holding period (12/31/1999–12/31/2020) of the tables showing withdrawals in Chapter 3. As a reminder, a single investment of $1 million was made at the beginning of the period. Withdrawals

---

1. Qualified distributions are generally withdrawals the Roth IRA owner makes (after age 59½) following a five-year period beginning with the first tax year for which a contribution was made to the Roth. If the distribution is not qualified, earnings may be subject to tax and a 10% early withdrawal penalty (under age 59½).

began at 4% ($40,000) of the initial investment, increasing by 3% annually. Withdrawals were made monthly on the last day of the month.

First, compare the Balanced Fund* without the effect of taxes to the Balanced Fund** with the effect of taxes. The 12/31/2020 value for the Balanced Fund* before taxes was roughly $2.3 million. After taxes, the Balanced Fund's** ending value was about $1.5 million. (You might reason that the difference between the two figures was paid out in taxes. Not so; keep in mind that market values were in flux during this period in time, including three bear markets, and withdrawals were occurring monthly. Taxes paid came to $320,339.)

Then, compare the S&P 500 Index Fund* without the effect of taxes ($205,698) to the S&P 500 Index Fund** after the effect of taxes ($47,000). Taxes came to $67,085. (You will also see a Short-Term Treasury Fund as a comparison.)

Table A 1999-2020 Before and After Taxes

For the Period 12/31/1999– 12/31/2020	Total Taxes Deducted & Paid	Total Dividend Income Reinvested	Total Capital Gains Reinvested	Total Withdrawals (4% of $1 million Start Value Increased Annually by 3%)	12/31/2020 Value	Total Return Annualized
Balanced Fund*	$0	$661,680	$639,715	$1,147,058	$2,261,852	7.8%
Balanced Fund**	$320,339	$556,405	$502,541	$1,147,058	$1,467,324	6.4%
S&P 500 Index Fund*	$0	$174,997	$0	$1,147,058	$205,698	2.4%
S&P 500 Index Fund**	$67,085	$160,945	$0	$1,147,058	$47,340	1.5%
Short-Term Treasury Fund*	$0	$464,271	$100,991	$1,147,058	$491,353	3.7%
Short-Term Treasury Fund**	$188,318	$413,717	$84,203	$1,147,058	$231,187	2.6%

Compare each fund without the effect of taxes to each fund with the effect of taxes. Tax rates are for a single filer earning $250,000 gross. (Federal Rate is 35%; Capital Gains Rate is 20%; State Rate is 6%.)

Source: Morningstar® Advisor Workstation^SM Hypothetical Tool

In Table A, notice the dividends and capital gains distributions for each fund. Those distributions help support the withdrawals in down market periods. The Balanced Fund's dividends and capital gains distributions were significantly higher than the dividends of the S&P 500 Index Fund, which had no capital gains distributions.

While each situation shown resulted in withdrawals of $1,147,058 over the period, the ending results were far different. The Balanced Fund before taxes returned 7.8% (see Balanced Fund*) and 6.4% after taxes (see Balanced Fund**). The S&P 500 Index Fund returned 2.4% before taxes (see S&P 500 Index Fund*), compared to 1.5% after taxes (see S&P 500 Index Fund**).

Appendix B
Mutual Fund Prospectus Disclosure of Share Classes

Sample disclosure of share classes from Investment Company of America Prospectus dated March 1, 2021, at https://www.capitalgroup.com/us/pdf /shareholder/mfgeprx-004_icap.pdf (pages 26–27)

"Factors you should consider when choosing a class of shares include:

- how long you expect to own the shares;
- how much you intend to invest;
- total expenses associated with owning shares of each class;
- whether you qualify for any reduction or waiver of sales charges (for example, Class A or 529-A or Class T or 529-T shares may be a less expensive option over time, particularly if you qualify for a sales charge reduction or waiver);
- whether you want or need the flexibility to effect exchanges among American Funds without the imposition of a sales charge (for example, while Class A shares offer such exchange privileges, Class T shares do not);
- whether you plan to take any distributions in the near future (for example, the contingent deferred sales charge will not be waived if you sell your Class 529-C shares to cover higher education expenses);
- and availability of share classes:
  - » Class C shares are not available to retirement plans that do not currently invest in such shares and that are eligible to invest in Class R shares, including retirement plans established under Internal Revenue Code Sections 401(a) (including 401(k) plans), 403(b) or 457;

» Class F and 529-F shares are available, as applicable, (i) to fee-based programs of investment dealers that have special agreements with the fund's distributor, (ii) to financial intermediaries that have been approved by, and that have special agreements with, the fund's distributor to offer Class F and 529-F shares to self-directed investment brokerage accounts that may charge a transaction fee, (iii) to certain registered investment advisors and (iv) to other intermediaries approved by the fund's distributor;

» Class F-3 shares (but not Class 529-F-3 shares) are also available to institutional investors, which include, but are not limited to, charitable organizations, governmental institutions and corporations. For accounts held and serviced by the fund's transfer agent the minimum investment amount is $1 million; and

» Class R shares are available (i) to retirement plans established under Internal Revenue Code Sections 401(a) (including 401(k) plans), 403(b) or 457, (ii) to nonqualified deferred compensation plans and certain voluntary employee benefit association and post-retirement benefit plans, (iii) to certain institutional investors (including, but not limited to, certain charitable organizations), (iv) to certain registered investment companies approved by the fund's investment adviser or distributor and (v) to other institutional-type accounts.

Each investor's financial considerations are different. You should speak with your financial professional to help you decide which share class is best for you."

Appendix C
How to Check Out Your Representative and Firm Using BrokerCheck

If you want to find out more information about an individual representative who works for a broker-dealer or investment adviser or dual registrant, you can do that using BrokerCheck, which is a free tool provided by FINRA (the Financial Industry Regulatory Authority). FINRA regulates the brokerage industry and coordinates disclosures for registered representatives of financial firms. At the site, you'll have the option of searching for details on a representative and the firm that employs him or her.

The Representative

To check out an individual, go to brokercheck.finra.org/. You'll see a tab called "Individual" and a tab called "Firm."

Click on the "Individual" tab and enter the individual's name or, if you have it, the broker's CRD (Central Registration Depository) number, which is a unique identifier issued by FINRA. You can also insert the name of the firm (optional) and the city, state, or ZIP code (also optional). Then, press the dark-blue "SEARCH" button to the right. (If the individual has a common name, you'll need his or her CRD number to refine the search.)

The results of the search will show you a box containing the individual's name and CRD number, the firm he or she works for, and its CRD number.

Pay attention to the circles that follow.

A light-blue circle with a "B" indicates the person's status as a broker; a dark-blue circle with an "IA" indicates that the person works for an investment adviser. If both circles appear, the person works for a dual registrant. You could also see a white circle with the letters "PR" for a previously registered broker or a previously registered investment adviser representative.

Further down the box, you'll see "disclosures," with a "yes" indicator (in gold) or a "no" indicator (in blue). Disclosures are "criminal matters, regulatory actions, civil judicial proceedings and financial matters in which the firm or one of its control affiliates has been involved."[1]

Further down again, you'll see "Years of Experience" and a figure representing the number of years the individual has worked in the industry.

Next is a very important box called "More Details." Don't skip this step. When you click on that box, you'll see a repeat of some of the earlier information. You'll see four large boxes:

1. A box called "Disclosure" (The color of the box will be either blue if the representative has no disclosures or gold if the representative has disclosures.)
2. A light-blue box for "Years of Experience" and "Firms" for the number of firms the individual has worked for
3. A green box for "Exams Passed"
4. A dark-blue box for "State Licenses"

Selecting each box one at a time will give you details.

When selecting the "Disclosures" category, it will show the date, type, and disposition of the issue. You can download a more detailed report (the link is above the company name on the right side of the page near the top, next to the "Share" icon) that will provide additional facts for consideration (for example, if there was a settlement involved, the dollar amount of the settlement).

When selecting "Years of Experience," you'll find a registration history that lays out graphically the various firms the individual worked for.

The "Licenses" section can be particularly informative when it involves a dual registrant, who might be licensed as a broker in a number of states, but as a dual registrant in fewer locations.

---

1. BrokerCheck Detailed Report, 3, https://brokercheck.finra.org/firm/summary/.

The "Examinations" section provides details on the licensing exams the individual has completed.

You will also want to know more about the firm the individual works for. To do that you'll select the "Firm" tab on BrokerCheck and enter the company's name (or better yet, CRD number, which is available on the right side of the page of the individual's report).

The Firm

Once entered, you'll find information on the firm that follows a somewhat similar format as just described with these exceptions. Only the first colored box (gold) is identical ("Disclosures").

You'll see four large boxes:

1. A box called "Disclosure"
2. A light-blue box for "SEC Registration Status" (including the date approved)
3. A green box for "Company Type" (corporation, for example)
4. A dark-blue box for the body that regulates the firm (SEC, for example) and the number of states where the firm is licensed

Again, selecting each box one at a time will give you details.

When selecting the "Disclosures" category, it will show you the total number of disclosures, their type (regulatory event, civil event, arbitration), and how many there are in each category. At the bottom of the section is a sentence stating:

"For details of these disclosures refer to the Detailed Report."

Clicking on the "Detailed Report" link will take you to an expanded look at the firm, including a full listing of the disclosure events. The opening page of the report's disclosure section details not only the categories for each event but also if they are pending, final, or on appeal. The subsequent pages will list each individual event and will include the current status of the disclosure, the allegations related to it, the resolution, and any possible sanctions.

When selecting "SEC Registration Status," you'll find information on the main office location and where (and what year) the company was established, along with the owners of the firm and its executive officers.

"Company Type" will take you to the same section, where you'll find "Type" under "Established In."

The "SEC" section details the states in which the firm is licensed, along with other registrations, including federal (for example, the SEC) and self-regulatory organizations (like FINRA or the New York Stock Exchange). The end of the section lists how many types of businesses the firm conducts, if it is affiliated with financial and investment institutions, and if it has referral or financial arrangements with other brokers or dealers. The downloadable Detailed Report digs deeper into those details through the "Firm Operations" section.

There is one other item of note: At the top right, next to the company's main address, is a blue button titled "Relationship Summary." Selecting that will give you the firm's CRS (Customer or Client Relationship Summary), the document we discussed in Chapter 12.

Appendix D
For Investment Advisers

Form ADV contains five parts[1]

1. Part 1A is for advisers filing with the SEC. Part 1A includes Disclosure Reporting Pages (DRPs) Part 1A Item 11. See Appendix E for DRP disclosure instructions. Part 1A is not required to be provided clients; it is available online through brokercheck.org.
2. Part 1B is for advisers filing with a state securities authority, not the SEC.
3. Part 2A (ADV Part 2A or the "Brochure") must be provided clients and prospective clients.
4. Part 2B (ADV Part 2B or the "Brochure Supplement") describes supervised persons and must also be provided clients and prospective clients.
5. Part 3 (ADV Part 3) is the Form CRS (2-4 pages) which must be provided clients and prospective clients.

---

1. General Instructions for Form ADV are found at https://www.sec.gov/about/forms/formadv-instructions.pdf.

Appendix E
DRP Instructions for ADV Part 1A (Item 11 Disclosure Information)

In this Item, we ask for information about your disciplinary history and the disciplinary history of all your advisory affiliates. We use this information to determine whether to grant your application for registration, to decide whether to revoke your registration or to place limitations on your activities as an investment adviser, and to identify potential problem areas to focus on during our on-site examinations. One event may result in "yes" answers to more than one of the questions below. In accordance with General Instruction 5 to Form ADV, "you" and "your" include the filing advisor and all relying advisors under an umbrella registration.

Your advisory affiliates are (1) all of your current employees (other than employees performing only clerical, administrative, support, or similar functions); (2) all of your officers, partners, or directors (or any person performing similar functions); and (3) all persons directly or indirectly controlling you or controlled by you. If you are a "separately identifiable department or division" (SID) of a bank, see the Glossary of Terms to determine who your advisory affiliates are.

If you are registered or registering with the SEC or if you are an exempt reporting adviser, you may limit your disclosure of any event listed in Item 11 to ten years following the date of the event. If you are registered or registering with a state, you must respond to the questions as posed; you may, therefore, limit your disclosure to ten years following the date of an event only in responding to Items 11.A.(1), 11.A.(2), 11.B.(1), 11.B.(2), 11.D.(4), and 11.H.(1)(a). For purposes of calculating this ten-year period, the date of an event is the date the final order, judgment, or decree was entered, or the date any rights of appeal from preliminary orders, judgments, or decrees lapsed.

You must complete the appropriate Disclosure Reporting Page (DRP) for "yes" answers to the questions in this Item 11.

Do any of the events below involve you or any of your supervised persons?

For "yes" answers to the following questions, complete a *Criminal Action DRP*:

   A. In the past ten years, have you or any advisory affiliate:
      (1) been convicted of or pled guilty or nolo contendere ("no contest") in a domestic, foreign, or military court to any felony?
      (2) been charged with any felony? (If you are registered or registering with the SEC, or if you are reporting as an exempt reporting adviser, you may limit your response to Item 11.A.(2) to charges that are currently pending.)
   B. In the past ten years, have you or any advisory affiliate:
      (1) been convicted of or pled guilty or nolo contendere ("no contest") in a domestic, foreign, or military court to a misdemeanor involving: investments or an investment related business, or any fraud, false statements, or omissions, wrongful taking of property, bribery, perjury, forgery, counterfeiting, extortion, or a conspiracy to commit any of these offenses?
      (2) been charged with a misdemeanor listed in Item 11.B.(1)? (If you are registered or registering with the SEC, or if you are reporting as an exempt reporting adviser, you may limit your response to Item 11.B.(2) to charges that are currently pending.)

For "yes" answers to the following questions, complete a *Regulatory Action DRP*:

   C. Has the SEC or the Commodity Futures Trading Commission (CFTC) ever:
      (1) found you or any advisory affiliate to have made a false statement or omission?
      (2) found you or any advisory affiliate to have been involved in a violation of SEC or CFTC regulations or statutes?

(3) found you or any advisory affiliate to have been a cause of an investment-related business having its authorization to do business denied, suspended, revoked, or restricted?

(4) entered an order against you or any advisory affiliate in connection with investment-related activity?

(5) imposed a civil money penalty on you or any advisory affiliate, or ordered you or any advisory affiliate to cease and desist from any activity?

D. Has any other federal regulatory agency, any state regulatory agency, or any foreign financial regulatory authority:

(1) ever found you or any advisory affiliate to have made a false statement or omission, or been dishonest, unfair, or unethical?

(2) ever found you or any advisory affiliate to have been involved in a violation of investment-related regulations or statutes?

(3) ever found you or any advisory affiliate to have been a cause of an investment-related business having its authorization to do business denied, suspended, revoked, or restricted?

(4) in the past ten years, entered an order against you or any advisory affiliate in connection with an investment-related activity?

(5) ever denied, suspended, or revoked your or any advisory affiliate's registration or license, or otherwise prevented you or any advisory affiliate, by order, from associating with an investment-related business or restricted your or any advisory affiliate's activity?

E. Has any self-regulatory organization or commodities exchange ever:

(1) found you or any advisory affiliate to have made a false statement or omission?

(2) found you or any advisory affiliate to have been involved in a violation of its rules (other than a violation designated as a "minor rule violation" under a plan approved by the SEC)?

(3) found you or any advisory affiliate to have been the cause of an investment-related business having its authorization to do business denied, suspended, revoked, or restricted?

(4) disciplined you or any advisory affiliate by expelling or suspending you or the advisory affiliate from membership, barring or suspending you or the advisory affiliate from association with other members, or otherwise restricting your or the advisory affiliate's activities?

F. Has an authorization to act as an attorney, accountant, or federal contractor granted to you or any advisory affiliate ever been revoked or suspended?

G. Are you or any advisory affiliate now the subject of any regulatory proceeding that could result in a "yes" answer to any part of Item 11.C., 11.D., or 11.E.?

<u>For "yes" answers to the following questions, complete a *Civil Judicial Action DRP*:</u>

H. (1) Has any domestic or foreign court:
    (a) in the past ten years, enjoined you or any advisory affiliate in connection with any investment-related activity?
    (b) ever found that you or any advisory affiliate were involved in a violation of investment-related statutes or regulations?
    (c) ever dismissed, pursuant to a settlement agreement, an investment-related civil action brought against you or any advisory affiliate by a state or foreign financial regulatory authority?
    (2) Are you or any advisory affiliate now the subject of any civil proceeding that could result in a "yes" answer to any part of Item 11.H.(1)?

<u>End of Item 11[1]</u>

---

1. "FORM ADV (Paper Version)" (SEC 2021), 23–27, https://www.sec.gov/about/forms/formadv-part1a.pdf.

Suggested Reading

The Classics

Graham, Benjamin. *The Intelligent Investor: A Book of Practical Counsel.* New York: HarperCollins, 1st ed. 1949/2003.

Graham, Benjamin, and David L. Dodd. *Security Analysis: Principles and Techniques.* New York: McGraw-Hill, 1st ed. 1934/2009.

Ibbotson, Roger G. *2021 SBBI® Yearbook Stocks, Bonds, Bills, and Inflation: U.S. Capital Markets Performance by Asset Class 1926–2020.* Illinois: Duff & Phelps, 2021.

Lefevre, Edwin. *Reminiscences of a Stock Operator: With New Commentary and Insights on the Life and Times of Jesse Livermore.* Hoboken, NJ: Wiley, 1st ed. 1923/2010.

Loeb, Gerald M. *The Battle for Stock Market Profits.* New York: Simon & Schuster, 1971.

Malkiel, Burton G. *A Random Walk Down Wall Street: The Time-Tested Strategy for Successful Investing.* New York: W.W. Norton, 1st ed. 1973/2019.

Markowitz, Harry M. *Portfolio Selection: Efficient Diversification of Investments*, 2nd ed. Massachusetts: Blackwell, 1st ed. 1959/1991.

O'Neil, William J. *How to Make Money in Stocks: A Winning System in Good Times or Bad.* New York: McGraw-Hill, 1st ed. 1988/2009.

Siegel, Jeremy J. *Stocks for the Long Run: The Definitive Guide to Financial Market Returns and Long-Term Investment Strategies.* New York: McGraw-Hill, 1st ed. 1994/2014.

Investing

"How to Read a Financial Statement," Economic Bulletin. XLVIII No. 8 (August, 2008). American Institute for Economic Research, https://www.aier.org/research/how-to-read-a-financial-statement/.

Benz, Christine. *Morningstar's 30-Minute Money Solutions: A Step-by-Step Guide to Managing Your Finances.* New Jersey: John Wiley & Sons, Inc., 2010.

Buffett, Sara, and Clark, David. *Buffettology: The Previously Unexplained Techniques That Have Made Warren Buffett the World's Most Famous Investor.* New York: Fireside, 1st ed. 1997/1999.

Cloonan, James B. *Investing at Level 3.* Illinois: American Association of Individual Investors, 2016.

Dorsey, Pat. *The Little Book That Builds Wealth: The Knockout Formula for Finding Great Investments.* New Jersey: Wiley, 2008.

Ellis, Charles D. and Burton Malkiel. *Winning the Loser's Game.* New York: McGraw Hill, 1st ed., 1998/2013.

Elmiger, Gregory, and Steve S. Kim. *RiskGrade Your Investments: Measure Your Risk and Create Wealth*. New Jersey: Wiley, 2003.

Elton, Edwin J., Gruber, Martin J., Brown, Stephen J., and Goetzmann, William N., *Modern Portfolio Theory and Investment Analysis*. New Jersey: Wiley, 9th ed., 2014.

Fisher, Philip A. *Common Stocks and Uncommon Profits and Other Writings*. New Jersey: John Wiley & Sons, 1st ed. 1996/2003.

Gitman, Lawrence J., et al. *Fundamentals of Investing*. 13th ed. Massachusetts: Prentice Hall, 2017.

Hackel, Kenneth S. *Security Valuation and Risk Analysis: Assessing Value in Investment Decision Making*. New York: McGraw-Hill, 2011.

Higgins, Robert C. *Analysis for Financial Management*, 12th ed., New York: McGraw Hill, 2019.

Hirt, Geoffrey A., and Stanley B. Block, *Fundamentals of Investment Management*, 10th ed. New York: McGraw-Hill, 2012.

Greenwald, Bruce C. N., et al. *Value Investing: From Graham to Buffett and Beyond*. New Jersey: Wiley, 2021.

Kelly, Jason. *The Neatest Little Guide to Stock Market Investing*. New York: Penguin, 1st ed. 1998/2013.

Leder, Michelle. *Financial Fine Print: Uncovering a Company's True Value*. New Jersey: Wiley, 2003.

Lynch, Peter. *Beating the Street*. New York: Fireside, 1st ed., 1993/1994.

Maginn, John L., et al. CFA Institute, *Managing Investment Portfolios: A Dynamic Process*. New Jersey: Wiley, 2007.

Morningstar Investor Workbook Series: Stocks Book 1: How Get Started in Stocks. New Jersey: Wiley, 2005.

Morningstar Investing Workbook Series: Stocks Book 2: How to Select Winning Stocks. New Jersey: Wiley, 2005.

Morningstar Investing Workbook Series: Stocks Book 3: How to Refine Your Stock Strategy. New Jersey: Wiley, 2005.

Newcomb, Sarah. *Loaded: Money, Psychology, and How to Get Ahead without Leaving Your Values Behind*, New Jersey: John Wiley & Sons, 2016.

Pinto, Jerald E., et al. CFA Institute. *Equity Asset Valuation*, 2nd ed. New Jersey: Wiley, 2010.

Shilling, A. Gary. *The Age of Deleveraging: Investment Strategies for a Decade of Slow Growth and Deflation*. New Jersey: Wiley, 2011.

Solin, Daniel R. *The Smartest Investment Book You'll Ever Read*. New York: Penguin, 1st ed. 2006/2010.

Stovall, Sam. *The Seven Rule of Wall Street: Crash Tested Investment Strategies that Beat the Market*. New York: McGraw-Hill Education, 2009.

Taleb, Nassim. *Fooled by Randomness: The Hidden Role of Chance in Life and in the Markets*. New York: Random House, 2004/2005.

Thau, Annette. *The Bond Book: Everything Investors Need to Know about Treasuries, Municipals, GNMAs, Corporates, Zeros, Bond Funds, Money Market Funds, and More*. New York: McGraw-Hill, 1st ed. 1992/2011.

Retirement, IRAs

Choate, Natalie B. *Life and Death Planning for Retirement Benefits. The Essential Handbook for Estate Planners.* Massachusetts: Ataxplan Publications, 8th ed. Revised 2019.

Giuliani, Peter. *Passing the Torch without Getting Burned*, Chicago: ABA Publishing, 2013.

Goldberg, Seymour, *A Professional's Guide to the IRA Distribution Rules Under the SECURE Act 2021* (ebook), https://leimbergservices.com/wdev/products.cfm?id=158.

Jason, Julie. *The Retirement Survival Guide: How to Make Smart Financial Decisions in Good Times and Bad.* New York: Sterling Publishing, 2017. Originally released as *The AARP Retirement Survival Guide: How to Make Smart Financial Decisions in Good Times and Bad.* New York: Sterling Publishing, 2009.

Jason, Julie. *Retire Securely: Insights on Money Management from an Award-Winning Financial Columnist.* New York: Sterling Publishing, 2018.

Pfau, Wade. *Retirement Planning Guidebook: Navigating the Important Decisions for Retirement Success.* Virginia: Retirement Researcher Media, 2021.

Slott, Ed. *The New Retirement Savings Time Bomb: How to Take Financial Control, Avoid Unnecessary Taxes, and Combat the Latest Threats to Your Retirement Savings.* New York: Penguin, 2021.

Zelinski, Ernie J., *How to Retire Happy, Wild, and Free.* Edmonton, AB, Canada: Visions International Publishing, 2015.

Social Security

Sacks, Avram. "Strategizing Your Social Security Claim," in *Second Acts for Solo and Small Firm Lawyers*, edited by Jennifer J. Rose, 193–230. Chicago: ABA Publishing, 2019.

Behavioral Finance

Baker, H. Kent and Victor Ricciardi. *Investor Behavior: The Psychology of Financial Planning and Investing.* New Jersey: John Wiley & Sons, 2014.

Belsky, Gary and Thomas Gilovich. *Why Smart People Make Big Money Mistakes and How to Correct Them: Lessons from the Life-Changing Science of Behavioral Economics.* New York: Simon & Schuster, 1st ed. 1999/2009.

Pompian, Sam M. *Behavioral Finance and Wealth Management: How to Build Optimal Portfolios That Account for Investor Biases.* New Jersey: Wiley, 2006.

Trading/Quantitative Strategies

Sipley, Richard. *Market Indicators: The Best-Kept Secret to More Effective Trading and Investing.* New York: Bloomberg Press, 2009.

Tortoriello, Richard. *Quantitative Strategies for Achieving Alpha.* New York: McGraw-Hill, 2009.

Zuckerman, Gregory. *The Man Who Solved the Market: How Jim Simons Launched the Quant Revolution.* New York: Penguin Random House LLC, 2019.

About the Author

Julie Jason, JD, LLM

Julie Jason began her Wall Street career as a securities lawyer (Assistant General Counsel for a major broker-dealer) and executive (president of the firm's managed futures subsidiary and of its trust company). In 1992, she founded Jackson, Grant Investment Advisers, Inc. of Stamford, CT, as an independent fiduciary stand-alone investment adviser. The firm specializes in managing retirement portfolios for high-net-worth and ultra-high-net-worth families.

Julie has the unique experience of having worked under two regulatory environments: on Wall Street with a registered broker-dealer regulated by the 1934 Act and on Main Street with a registered investment adviser regulated by the Advisers Act.

A long-time advocate for financial literacy education, her award-winning books and columns are referenced at www.juliejason.com. Her work has received recognition for clarity, accuracy and excellence in financial literacy education. As a volunteer, for three years she served as the representative of the state of Connecticut before the Taxpayer Advocacy Panel, the federal advisory committee to the IRS, earning President Obama's Call to Service Award. She and her family reside in Greenwich, Connecticut. Her biography is published in *Who's Who in American Law*, *Who's Who in America*, and *Who's Who in the World*.

Acknowledgments

Truth be told, work on this book began in the summer of 2018 in Nantucket on a three-generational people-packed vacation. Proposed regulations had just been released by the U.S. Securities and Exchange Commission (SEC) that would help investors better understand the disparate members of the financial services industry, enough so to choose wisely for their needs—and I was captivated.

While I was not aware at the time that I was preparing anything other than the comment letter I submitted later that summer, in retrospect I see that I was gearing up to write this book, a three-year project if measured from 2018.

So, in a way, *The Discerning Investor* owes its place in ABA publishing history to the SEC. The regulations and disclosures will help investors make more informed decisions. Investors will be more able to recognize and perhaps escape conflicts of interest. They will understand better what to make of services and service providers, avoiding miscues due simply to lack of awareness, especially during those heightened-risk times of transition from work to retirement. Thank you, SEC, for providing investors Form CRS and best interest regulations.

As to the subject of retirement investing, I have to thank my clients and the many people who initiated contact with me over the years as a result of my lectures and writings. I have been privileged to witness many successes and to recognize when things might go awry. It is this experience gained over three decades that helped shape Parts II and IV of the book.

Likewise, over the years and particularly with this manuscript, many experts offered guidance and resources, which I reference in the book, among them, Capital Group, CFRA, Ibbotson's SBBI Yearbooks, J.P. Morgan Asset Management, Morningstar, Inc., S&P Global Dow Jones Indices, and STEELE Software, as well as individuals who shared insights and critiques: namely, lawyers Cliff Alexander, Manny Bernardo, Cliff Ennico,

James Gust, David Lehn, JoAnn Luehring, Rick Ryder, Jay Sandak, Max Schatzow, Steve Seckler; CPAs Russell Abrahms and Tony Aiken; market experts Charles Rotblut and Sam Stovall; longtime friends Nina Streitfeld and Charles Zatzkin; plus a special thank you goes to former SEC chairmen Jay Clayton and Harvey Pitt. Your generosity in sharing your time and expertise is, as always, genuinely appreciated.

The research, fact-checking, and review process was the work of my Jackson, Grant colleagues, who cannot be thanked enough for their tireless dedication to the book: Sarah Beyrich, Bob Carroll, Janella Joyner Delva, Ryan Flynn, Angela Gagliardo, Ilona Kucharczyk, Chris Richcreek, and Michael Tenreiro. Thank you all for your fealty to *The Discerning Investor*, the firm, and to all the clients who you serve with even greater commitment.

Finally, there was someone behind the scenes who patiently and carefully guided me with comments and questions during the evolution of the manuscript. That someone is Sarah Craig, the American Bar Association's executive editor, easily the best editor I've worked with.

All of you . . . and many more who are unnamed . . . including my children, grandchildren, cousins, close friends, my fiancé, and my late mother (a retired physician who faithfully read *The Economist* every week and almost made it to the book's finish). You who lived through those weekends and evenings and would-be vacations . . . you deserve my gratitude, well beyond what words can convey.

My sincere thanks to you all.

It is my hope that *The Discerning Investor* will serve those lawyers, both young and old, who want to retire financially secure—and those who want their retirements to be, in Ernie Zelinski's words, "happy, wild and free."[1]

---

1. Ernie J. Zelinski is the author of the best-selling book, "How to Retire Happy, Wild and Free: Retirement Wisdom That You Won't Get from Your Financial Advisor."

Index